Specification and Management of a Cable Infrastructure

IT Infrastructure Library

Ray Harris
Jonathan Harker

Riverwalk House,
157-161 Millbank
London, SW1P 4RT

LONDON: HMSO

© Copyright: Controller of HMSO, 1991

First published: 1991

ISBN: 0 11 330552 4

This is one of the books published in the IT Infrastructure Library series. At regular intervals, further books will be published and the Library will be completed by early 1992. Since many customers would like to receive the IT Infrastructure Library books automatically on publication, a standing order service has been set up. For further details on standing orders please contact:

HMSO Publicity (P9D), FREEPOST, Norwich, NR3 1BR
(*No stamp needed for UK customers*).

Until the whole Library is published, and subject to availability, draft copies of unpublished books may be obtained from CCTA if you are a standing order customer. To obtain drafts please contact:

Environmental Infrastructure Services
CCTA
Riverwalk House, 157-161 Millbank
London SW1P 4RT.

For further information on other CCTA products, contact

Press and Public Relations,
CCTA
Riverwalk House, 157-161 Millbank
London SW1P 4RT.

This document has been produced using procedures conforming to
BSI 5750 Part 1: 1987; ISO 9001: 1987.

Table of Contents

1.	**Management summary**	**1**
2.	**Introduction**	**3**
2.1	Purpose	3
2.2	Target readership	3
2.3	Scope	4
2.4	Related guidance	5
2.5	Standards	7
2.6	Referenced documents	9
2.7	Definition of terms	9
3.	**Project management and liaison**	**11**
3.1	Beginning a cable infrastructure project	11
3.2	Project team responsibilities	11
3.3	Project management techniques	14
3.4	Contributors to the specification	20
3.5	Influences of the IS strategy	22
3.6	Strategic constraints on the specification	23
4.	**Cable infrastructure management**	**25**
4.1	The cable infrastructure as an asset	25
4.2	Configuration management	26
4.3	Change control procedures	26
4.4	Use of the help desk	27
4.5	Auditing	29
4.6	Component identification	29
4.7	Incident reporting and logging	31
4.8	Maintenance	33
4.9	Managing cables carrying sensitive data	35
4.10	Recording logical and physical relationships	36
4.11	Resilience and contingency measures	36
4.12	Resources	37

IT Infrastructure Library
Specification and Management of a Cable Infrastructure

5.	**Reliability and resilience**	**39**
5.1	The importance of availability	39
5.2	Quality and availability requirements	41
5.3	Specifying for reliability and resilience	42
5.4	Maintenance	44
5.5	Costs and benefits of reliability and resilience	46
6.	**Quantification**	**47**
6.1	Quantification has become important	47
6.2	Objectives	47
6.3	Connection quantification	48
6.4	Media quantification	49
6.5	Presentation quantification	51
7.	**Cable topologies**	**53**
7.1	Topologies should be strategic	53
7.2	Physical cable topology	53
7.3	Logical topology	55
7.4	Sensitivities	59
7.5	Sources of further information	62
8.	**Physical cabling options and design**	**63**
8.1	Cable media options	63
8.2	Voice wiring design	64
8.3	Data wiring design	66
8.4	Fibre-optics	67
8.5	Coaxial cable	71
8.6	Shielded twisted pair	74
8.7	Unshielded twisted pair	75
8.8	Ribbon cable	77
9.	**Accommodation requirements**	**79**
9.1	Accommodation must be planned and specified	79
9.2	Cable entry points	79
9.3	Vertical cable distribution	80

9.4	Horizontal cable distribution	83
9.5	Communications closets	85
9.6	Equipment rooms and work space	86
9.7	New buildings	88
9.8	The constraints of existing old buildings	89
9.9	Sources of further information	90
10.	**Provision of environmental services**	**91**
10.1	Services and cable infrastructures	91
10.2	Power, heating, ventilation, and air conditioning	92
10.3	Electromagnetic interference	94
10.4	Earthing	95
10.5	Fire protection	96
10.6	Security	97
10.7	Lighting	98
10.8	Further information	98
11.	**The structure of the Operational Requirement**	**99**
11.1	Why use an Operational Requirement?	99
11.2	What makes a good OR?	100
11.3	What should an OR look like?	100
11.4	Setting the scene	101
11.5	Stating the requirement	103
11.6	Rules for suppliers	106
11.7	Related guides	109
12.	**Evaluation**	**111**
12.1	Obtaining value for money requires evaluation	111
12.2	Planning the evaluation process	111
12.3	Evaluation criteria	112
12.4	Shortlisting	115
12.5	Evaluating tenders	116
13.	**Commissioning and acceptance testing**	**119**
13.1	Why, who and when?	119

13.2	Details of the test procedure	120
13.3	Details of the tests	121
13.4	Sampling	124

14. Standards — 125

14.1	The use of standards	125
14.2	Sources of Standards, guides and regulations	125
14.3	International Standards, guides and regulations	126
14.4	National Standards, guides and regulations	127
14.5	Emerging standards	128
14.6	*De facto* standards	129

15. Management of the installation of cables — 131

15.1	Installation management must be carefully planned	131
15.2	Co-ordination with fitting out	132
15.3	Sequencing installation	134
15.4	Timescales	135

16. Cable management tools — 137

16.1	The need for cable management tools	137
16.2	What tools are available?	137
16.3	Resources	141
16.4	Limitations and costs	141

17. Benefits, costs and possible problems — 143

17.1	Benefits available	143
17.2	The costs of specification and management	143
17.3	Possible problems	145

18. Bibliography — 147

| 18.1 | CCTA | 147 |
| 18.2 | Other publications | 147 |

Annex A. Glossary of terms — A1

Annex B. GOSIP cabling strategy — B1

Foreword

Welcome to the IT Infrastructure Library module on **Specification and Management of a Cable Infrastructure.**

This module is one of a series in the Environmental Sets of the Library. In their respective areas the IT Infrastructure Library publications complement and provide more detail than the IS Guides.

The ethos behind the development of the IT Infrastructure Library is the recognition that organizations are becoming increasingly dependent on IT in order to satisfy their corporate aims and meet their business needs. This growing dependency leads to growing requirements for quality IT services. Quality means 'matched to business needs and user requirements as these evolve'.

The publications forming the major part of the Library are a series of codes of practice intended to facilitate the quality management of IT services and of the IT Infrastructure. (By IT Infrastructure, we mean an organization's computers and networks - hardware, software and computer related communications, upon which application systems and IT services are built and run). The codes of practice will assist organizations to provide quality IT services in the face of skill shortages, system complexity, rapid change, current and future user requirements, growing user expectations, etc. Details of these modules are available from CCTA Infrastructure Management Services in Gildengate House.

Supporting the IT Infrastructure is the Environmental Infrastructure. It is recognized that environmental issues, from building specification to the practicalities of cable distribution, lighting, noise, power, etc, are less well understood in IT service organizations than the IT and its infrastructure. However these issues can be just as important in delivering a quality IT service.

The Environmental Sets of modules provide guidance on addressing environmental issues. Their aim is to assist the implementation and management of an environmental infrastructure to support the needs of an organization's IT services.

IT Infrastructure Library
Specification and Management of a Cable Infrastructure

Each module commences with a **Management summary** aimed at senior managers (Directors of IT and above, typically down to Civil Service Grade 5), senior IT staff and, in some cases, users or office managers (typically Civil Service Grades 5 to 7). The target readership for the main text is variable and identified in the **Introduction** section of each module. Wherever possible technical detail is confined to annexes.

If you have any comments on this or other modules, do please let us know. A **Comments sheet** is provided with every module. Alternatively you may wish to contact us directly using the reference points given in **Further information**.

Acknowledgement

The assistance of Jonathan Harker (under contract to CCTA from Butler Cox) is gratefully acknowledged.

Section 1
Management summary

1. Management summary

Aim of the module

This module gives guidance on the planning, specification, evaluation and management of a building cable infrastructure for IT, complementing the **Cable Infrastructure Strategy** module which propounds the arguments for strategic cabling and provides guidance on the formulation of a cable infrastructure strategy. For those organizations who are implementing a GOSIP-based network strategy, this module provides guidance on the implementation of strategic cabling options described in the supplement to GOSIP Version 3.1; for ease of reference the GOSIP cabling strategy is reproduced at Annex B.

Strategic cabling (the installation of a building-wide cabling infrastructure to specified strategic networking standards) enables IT services to be delivered effectively and efficiently, whilst offering long-term savings over tactical cabling (installing only those cables required to meet specific requirements as and when equipment is installed). Strategic cabling has become widely recognized as the best method of providing communications services, within a building, to support the business needs of an organization.

Readership

The intended readers of this module are those who would be involved in the specification and management of a building cable infrastructure including IS managers, IT project managers and Cabling Managers. Other IT specialists may also find the module, or parts of it, of benefit in ascertaining the implications of implementing a strategic cabling infrastructure.

Content of the module

The guidance covers a wide variety of topics relevant to the installation and ongoing management of a cable infrastructure. Topics include:

* the identification of physical options and topologies for cabling

* the relationship between cabling and other building services and the potential constraints that buildings may impose

* procurement considerations, including Operational Requirement and evaluation

* the management of the installation project, acceptance and the ongoing operation of the cable infrastructure.

The IT Infrastructure Library
Specification and Management of a Cable Infrastructure

Benefits

The module is a comprehensive guide on the subject matter. However it is not aimed only at large organizations. The general principles are applicable to any size of organization.

The benefits available from following the guidance presented in this module include:

* reducing the time and cost of implementing changes in configuration and location of IT

* the economics of a cable infrastructure matched to the business needs of the organization

* protecting the investment made by sound management control of the infrastructure.

Resources

The module emphasizes that for a cable infrastructure project to succeed, adequate resources need to be identified and allocated to:

* establishing a project team with the necessary expertise

* identifying the requirements of the organization

* producing the Operational Requirement

* managing the procurement

* managing implementation and acceptance

* establishing ongoing operational management.

Recommendations

The key recommendations are that:

* early planning of the infrastructure is essential. Many aspects must be considered, including the corporate IS strategy, necessary works services, occupancy timescales and emerging standards

* liaison with building specifiers must be established, such as architects and space planners, to ensure that all physical implications are addressed

* commitment is required at all levels if the implementation and operation are to be successful

* cable management procedures and tools should be specified and procured as a part of the infrastructure project, and put in place prior to cable installation, to allow the configuration database to be built up within the acceptance procedures.

2. Introduction

2.1 Purpose

The IT Infrastructure Library module **Cable Infrastructure Strategy**, which complements the guidance given in this module, was written to raise the awareness of the importance of an organization's developing a cable strategy, through its key message:

"flexible, adaptable, and maintainable cable infrastructures will alleviate, if not obviate, the problems associated with tactical cabling."

The implementation of a cable strategy is often a major undertaking and must be regarded as a project in its own right.

This module is a practical guide to planning, specifying and managing a cable infrastructure installation project. Guidance is provided on the necessary stages of the project from determining the specification, through procurement, installation and commissioning, to the ongoing management requirements.

The user of this module should be familiar with the organization's cabling strategy, which is an essential reference when planning and specifying cable infrastructure requirements.

2.2 Target readership

This module is aimed primarily at those involved in the decision-making and management processes of an infrastructure project including:

* IS Managers
* IT Project Managers and Cabling Managers
* IT specialists within the organization.

The function of cable management may be a single responsibility during the specification and implementation of a cable infrastructure. Once the infrastructure is accepted, the ongoing duties of the Cabling Manager will fall under the configuration management function, actual responsibility being determined by the anticipated activity on the cable infrastructure.

The secondary readership of the module is other members of the cable infrastructure project team who will influence the specification or management processes - for example:

* Consultants
* Architects
* Accommodation Officers.

2.3 Scope

A cable infrastructure consists of all the cables in a building, including power, telecommunications, security, safety, and environmental control systems, and the accommodation provided for them. The cable infrastructure includes:

* inter-building cabling (campus)
* cables entering or leaving the building
* intra-building cabling (backbone and horizontal)
* cable and closet space throughout the building.

2.3.1 Planning and specification considerations

To implement a strategic cable infrastructure, there are many factors to be considered. These include:

* initial and future communications and power requirements of the users
* the implications of standards and codes of practice
* safety and security, of persons, property and data
* the flexibility, availability, adaptability and resilience required
* constraints imposed by the suitability of the buildings for strategic cabling
* contingency plans to implement in the event of a disaster.

This module concentrates on the specification and management of power (for IT), voice and data cabling only. However, the relationships to other infrastructure aspects, such as building services and security installations, and the benefits to be gained from adopting the outlined approach are also included.

The main guidance provided is towards the development of a specification for:

* the cable infrastructure Operational Requirement (OR) (section 11)
* the management procedures (section 15), controls and tools (section 16)
* commissioning and acceptance testing (section 13).

Potential benefits, costs and possible problems associated with the specification and management of a cable infrastructure are also illustrated (section 17).

2.3.2 Management considerations

Management commitment is vital to ensure that the objectives of the cable strategy are realized, and it is important that the organization appreciates that this management role will continue beyond the completion of the installation. Without ongoing support, an infrastructure will rapidly become unmanageable and the investment will be jeopardized. The cost of regaining control is likely to be substantial.

Owing to the relevance of cabling to the IS strategy and the investment required, senior management will be involved in the early decision processes of the Cable Infrastructure project. However, longer-term commitment is also required in resourcing the management of the infrastructure, to ensure that the investment is protected and the potential benefits are realized. The cabling is a fundamental element of the strategic IT infrastructure and must be managed in a way that reflects its importance.

If the approach detailed in this module is to be followed successfully, the organization must already have in place an IT Infrastructure strategy. This strategy should include communications requirements in terms of strategic LAN standards and the future requirements for voice and data communications.

2.4 Related guidance

The following modules are relevant and the reader is referred to these for additional information on specific topics.

Accommodation Specification

Provides guidance on the preparation of an Accommodation Brief for a computer centre.

Availability Management	Provides guidance on the planning and maintenance of IT systems, and on the recovery of failed systems, to ensure that availability and reliability of IT services to users is in accordance with service level agreements.
Cable Infrastructure Strategy	Considers strategic issues, and the costs and benefits of planning, installing and maintaining a cable infrastructure.
Change Management	Covers management of change, from impact assessment through to authorization, building and implementation.
Computer Installation and Acceptance	Gives advice on how to install and accept new computers and computer equipment.
Environmental Services Strategy	Outlines a strategy that will ensure the environmental services in buildings, which support IT facilities, can be upgraded from the initial requirement to the ultimate level of service which the occupier may require, without disrupting the IT services.
Fire Precautions in IT Installations	Provides guidance on fire precautions for IT equipment installed in the office as well as the computer centre.
Help Desk	Gives guidance on the role of the Help Desk to provide support to users, particularly when there are IT service incidents. The planning and control of the Help Desk function are also included.
Management of Electrical Interference	Describes the detrimental effect of electrical interference on IT equipment and the preventive measures that can be applied.
Managing a Quality Working Environment for IT Users	Provides guidance on a range of ergonomic and environmental problems encountered in the office and recommends solutions.
Management of Local Processors and Terminals	Provides guidance on the plans and controls needed to manage computers located in users' premises. The aim is to control all aspects of IT assets and so provide the conditions for quality IT service to be made available economically and effectively.
Modular Computer Buildings	Reviews the design, construction and performance of modular (computer) buildings
Network Management	Provides guidance on how to plan and manage telecommunications networks. The aim is to make sure that organizations' networks are managed as an integral part of their IT infrastructures, with a view to providing the required quality of IT services across the whole network.

Office Design and Planning	Provides guidance on the design, planning and furnishing of an office to support users and use space effectively.
Problem Management	Covers the management of incidents (interruptions to the normal expected behaviour of IT services), problems (the causes, as yet undiagnosed, of incidents) and errors (the causes, once diagnosed).
Secure Power Supplies	Examines the issues to be considered to achieve a totally secure power supply system.
Service Level Management	Describes the use and management of service level agreements, which formalize the users' and IT services group's expectations of quality of IT services to be provided.

2.5 Standards

2.5.1 Introduction

Throughout the module appropriate reference is made to standards when relevant to the subject matter. Section 14 provides a detailed summary of standards, regulations and guidelines applicable to a cabling infrastructure. Standards, whether organizational, de facto or de jure - national or international - are fundamental for any enabling infrastructure. For a cable infrastructure the networking standards, both current and projected, of the organization are an essential element in the specification of that infrastructure.

There is currently considerable activity within the standards community in the development of an international standard for customer premises cabling. Although much valuable drafting work has been undertaken, of which extensive use has been made in the formulation of de facto standards, the promulgation of an approved international standard is not imminent. Such a standard will be complementary to those networking standards which form the basis of the ISO 7-layer model for Open System Interconnection (OSI).

2.5.2 GOSIP

UK GOSIP (Government OSI Profile) provides the standards framework on which the networking elements of an IT infrastructure are based. It is founded on the premise that the base OSI standards developed by the international standards bodies are, by definition, very broad in scope and sphere of application and thus, on their own, not sufficiently precise to meet the objectives of:

* facilitating procurement and acceptance testing of communications-based products

* ensuring that different, and separately procured, systems can interwork to an assured level of functionality

* providing a clear specification to manufacturers on which to base strategic product development.

GOSIP is therefore a selection, or profile, of OSI protocols for a particular user environment - that is, UK government administrative IT services - and seen as an essential step in the practical application of OSI. However this environment does not differ greatly from that of many organizations in the private sector and the public availability of the GOSIP specification works to the mutual benefit of IT suppliers, government and commerce.

As the GOSIP specification developed, requests for guidance on the physical media for the interconnection of GOSIP based products increased. The absence of stable, internationally-agreed, Standards militated against a formal cabling subprofile on which a procurement specification could be based. The supplement to Version 3.1 of GOSIP, published in February 1990, provided guidance on cabling options for organizations who were basing their network strategies on GOSIP standards.

It is not intended to issue a supplement with future versions of GOSIP. By addressing topics that were not within the domain of stable international standards the supplement was beyond the scope of the GOSIP Specification. However, for those organizations who are implementing GOSIP-based network strategies, the information contained in the GOSIP V3.1 Supplement will continue to provide useful reference material for determining the requirements for specification of a cabling infrastructure, in support of the guidance contained in this module. Chapter 6 (Cabling Strategy) of the GOSIP V3.1 Supplement is reproduced, in its entirety, as Annex B.

Section 2
Introduction

This module, however, is not intended to be GOSIP specific and the guidance is equally applicable to other strategies.

2.6 Referenced documents

Sources of information used in the compilation of this module, together with other material which complements it, are included in Section 18, Bibliography.

2.7 Definition of terms

Throughout this module, reference is made to the local area network (LAN) Standards of Ethernet and Token Ring. In the context of this module, Ethernet refers to ISO 8802/3 networks, and Token Ring refers to ISO 8802/5 networks. The specifier should be aware that some proprietary implementations of Ethernet are standard compatible, not fully compliant, with ISO 8802/3. The implication is that, while products conforming to standards will operate over a compliant LAN, one vendor's compatible products may not support those of another vendor.

Terms and acronyms used in this module are defined in Annex A, Glossary of terms.

The IT Infrastructure Library
Specification and Management of a Cable Infrastructure

Section 3
Project management and liaison

3. Project management and liaison

3.1 Beginning a cable infrastructure project

With any large project, it is essential that effort is put in at the very beginning. Two key areas that should be addressed at the beginning of an infrastructure project are establishing the project management structures and procedures, and identifying the inputs to, and constraints on, the project.

A cable infrastructure project will normally involve many people, with a wide variety of skills and responsibilities, and both internal and external to the organization. In addition, the project may continue over a prolonged period: two years or more is common.

This section of the module introduces:

* the CCTA's project management methodology, PRINCE (Projects IN Controlled Environments)

* an approach to identifying and managing liaison with project personnel

* the strategic constraints that will shape the specification of the cable infrastructure.

3.2 Project team responsibilities

PRINCE

CCTA has developed a structured set of procedures, known as PRINCE, specifically designed for managing projects in IS/IT environments. CCTA has made PRINCE publicly available; no licence is required for its use. Further information on PRINCE will be found in the PRINCE reference manuals.

Key personnel

At the start of a project, it is important to identify the key personnel who will take management responsibility for the project.

Project structure

One of the five components in PRINCE is organization; a structure is set out for the project roles from the most senior to the most junior. PRINCE requires the establishment of:

* a Project Board, to manage the project for its whole duration, representing the three senior management roles of the IT Executive, the business and its users, and technical responsibilities

- a Project Assurance Team, also appointed for the duration of the project, with representation from the business, technical and user communities

- a Project Manager, appointed for the duration of the project, to:
  - plan and define the responsibilities of each stage manager
  - ensure that the project progresses to time and budget
  - report to the Project Board
  - manage the interface with the outside world (Further information is given below)

- Stage Managers (could be the Project Manager for one stage projects) appointed for each stage (see Section 3.3), to ensure that the stage deliverables are produced to time, within budget and to acceptable quality standards (Further information is given below)

- Stage Teams, created during each stage, to implement the project.

This organization is shown in figure 1, opposite.

Project Manager

A key role is that of the Project Manager, who has the responsibility for forming the individuals nominated for the project into cohesive teams, and for motivating them to achieve the desired results. The Project Manager should therefore have a good grasp of the human side of a project. They should generate enthusiasm through being seen to be involved, and should be sympathetic and receptive to problems and suggestions.

Further definition of the responsibilities of each group, and how they interact, are detailed in the PRINCE reference manuals.

Stage Teams

The Stage Teams for a cable infrastructure project will usually include representation from the four groups concerned with and affected by the project:

- the organization's technical staff
- vendors and installers of the infrastructure components
- professional advisers - for example, architects, M & E consultants and management consultants

Section 3
Project management and liaison

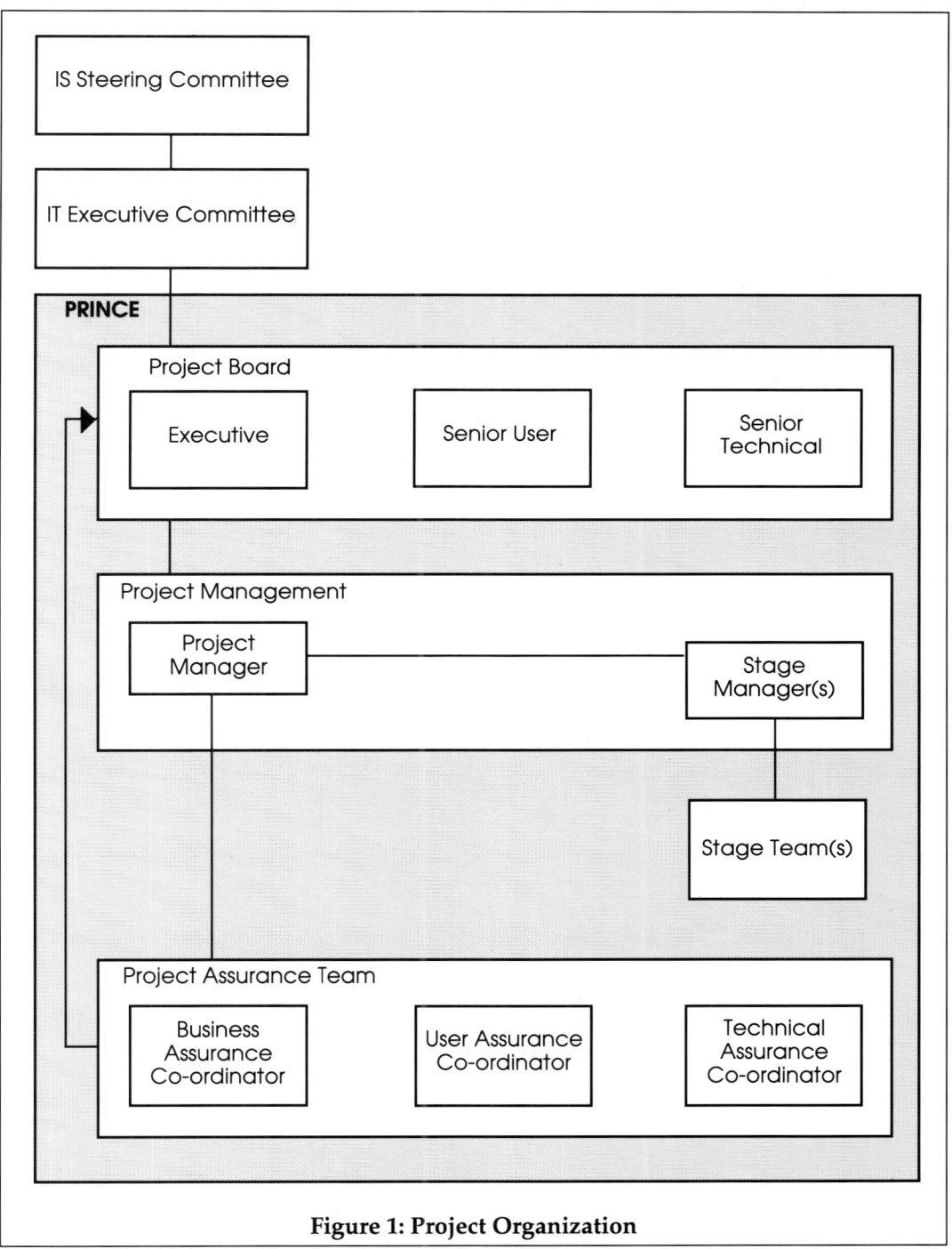

Figure 1: Project Organization

* senior users representing the business areas and all users of the system.

Involving the users

End-user involvement in projects which involve extensive works services is important. In the past, user participation in projects has been limited, with decisions being made by technical groups and specialists. However, it is now accepted that people have a greater commitment to change when they have been involved in the decision-making process. Including senior users on the project board should therefore contribute to the success of a project by ensuring that:

* the user requirements are accurately defined
* the user expectations are realistic
* potential business or user problems are identified and resolved at an early stage.

3.3 Project management techniques

Stages and tasks

An established approach to managing a large project is to break it down into many stages, each made up of small self-contained tasks, and to allocate these tasks to individuals or small teams.

Within PRINCE, each stage ends at a point where a decision must be made either to continue to the next stage, or to abandon (or defer) the project. There will be a minimum of two stages to a project - project planning and project implementation. An end-stage assessment is required at the completion of each stage.

Checkpoints

Key events in a project will occur during a stage, such as the completion of the delivery of equipment to site or of cabling on a particular floor. These points, which do not have any duration or activity themselves, are known as Checkpoints and act as control points for the Project Manager and targets for the project teams.

Section 3
Project management and liaison

The project management method must allow a large number of tasks to be managed simultaneously during a stage, monitoring deliverables against the resources allocated, while maintaining an overall view of the project. The impact on the project Checkpoints of any variance in one task should be apparent, so that the project management resources are applied to those tasks critical to the overall success of the project.

Planning

Plans, which must be in writing, will be prepared at two levels: project plans and stage plans. Each will include technical plans (what, when, how), and resource plans (who, how much).

Project management software

The Project Manager is faced with a bewildering choice of software packages for project management and control, ranging from simple PC-based products to programs running on mainframe computers. Most, however, provide versions of the standard project management techniques of Project Networks (or critical path diagrams), Gantt Charts and Resource Histograms.

To provide a standardized package including these techniques, CCTA has produced a software package designed to support the planning and control concepts of the PRINCE project management methodology on a PC. Specified and designed by CCTA, ADEPT-2 (A Decision Environment for PRINCE Tasks) was implemented by Metier Management Systems Ltd using Artemis 2000. Figures 2 to 5 are examples of ADEPT-2 outputs, which are given overleaf.

The IT Infrastructure Library
Specification and Management of a Cable Infrastructure

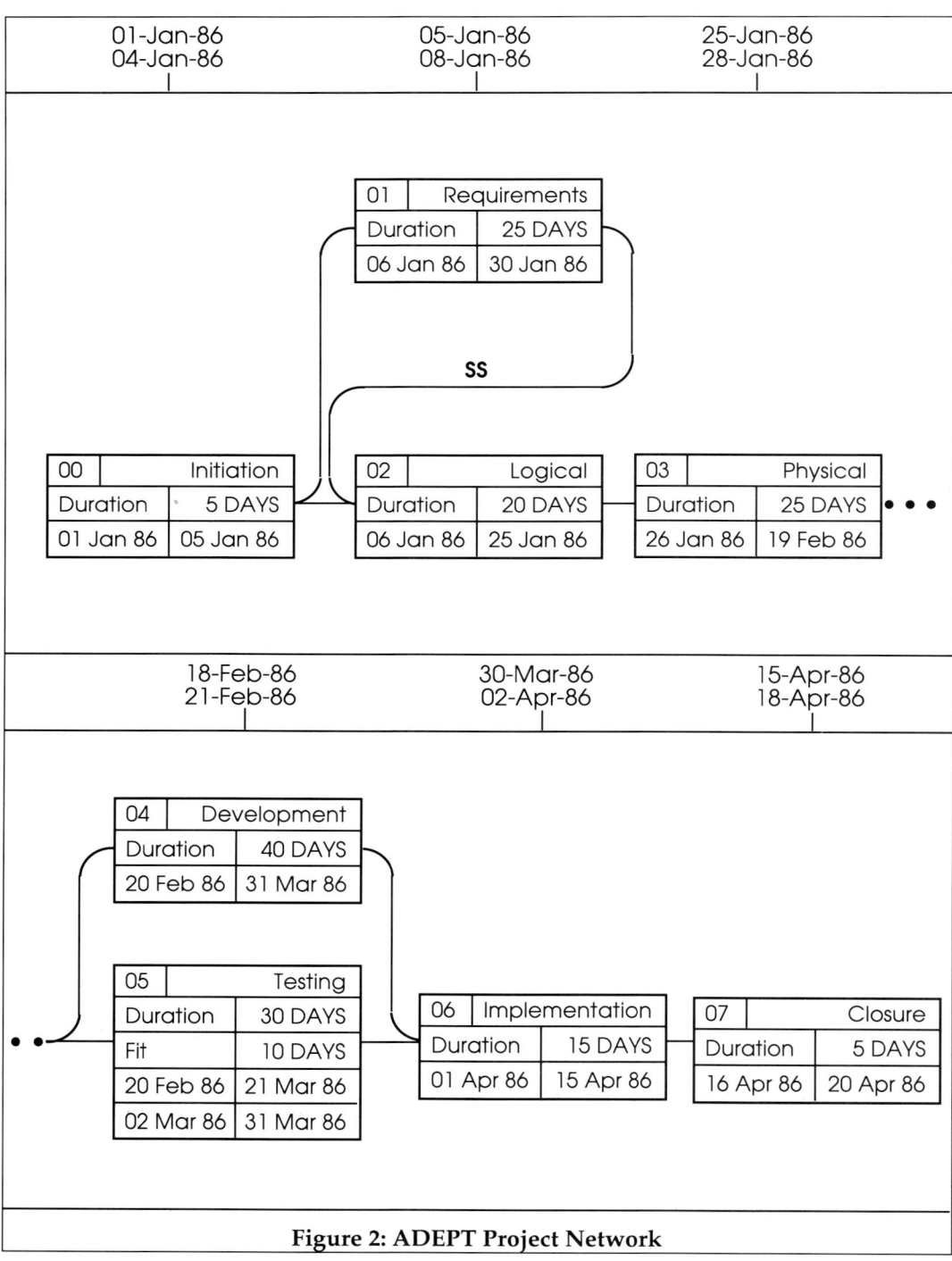

Figure 2: ADEPT Project Network

Section 3
Project management and liaison

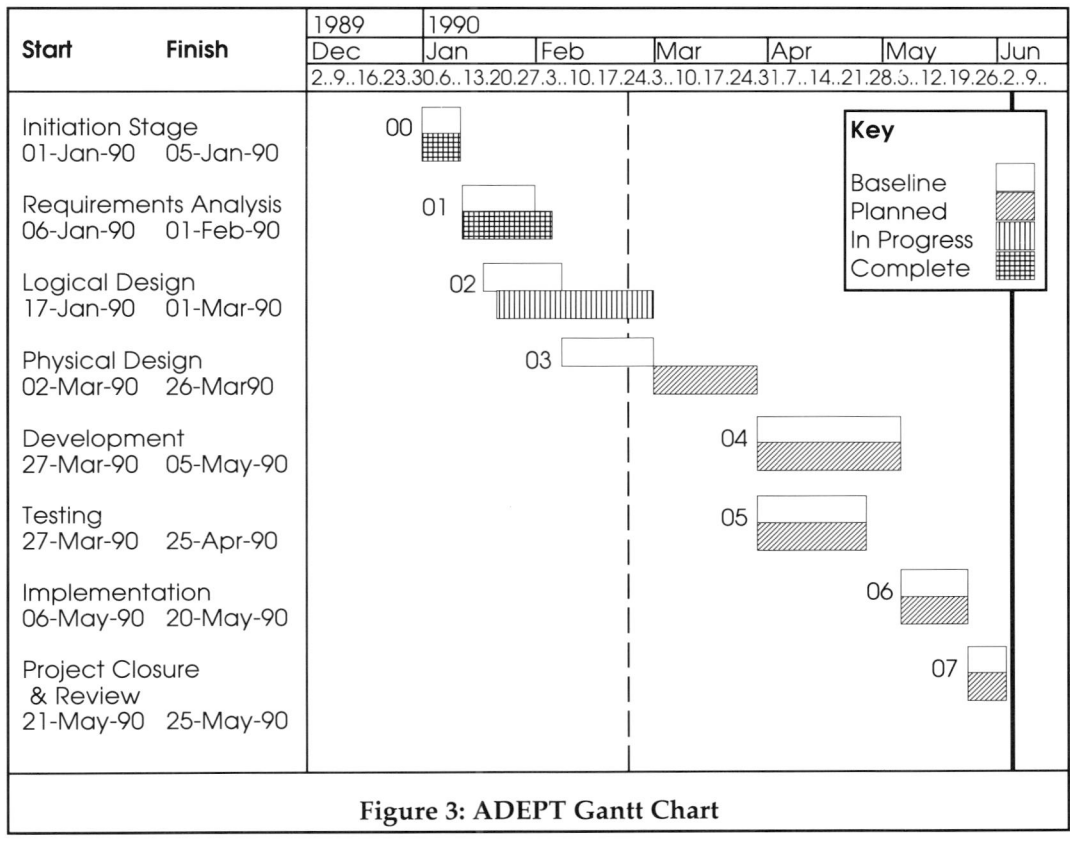

Figure 3: ADEPT Gantt Chart

Project network

Figure 2 illustrates a simple project network. The project network illustrates all the tasks in a project in chronological order showing the interdependencies between related tasks, the project checkpoints and the project stages. The tasks are shown with their durations, enabling a critical path to be denoted where slippage in a task will result in delay to the project (unless subsequent critical tasks are compressed). The effects of slippage in non-critical tasks may be to make them critical, giving revised or multiple critical paths.

Gantt Chart

A Gantt Chart, figure 3 above, shows actual progress against plan on a bar chart. Project checkpoints, and slippage, are clearly shown. The PRINCE manuals emphasize that amendments to the chart must not hide or alter the originally agreed plan. Many projects have been completed exactly to (the latest) plan, but with cost and time overruns against the original budgets.

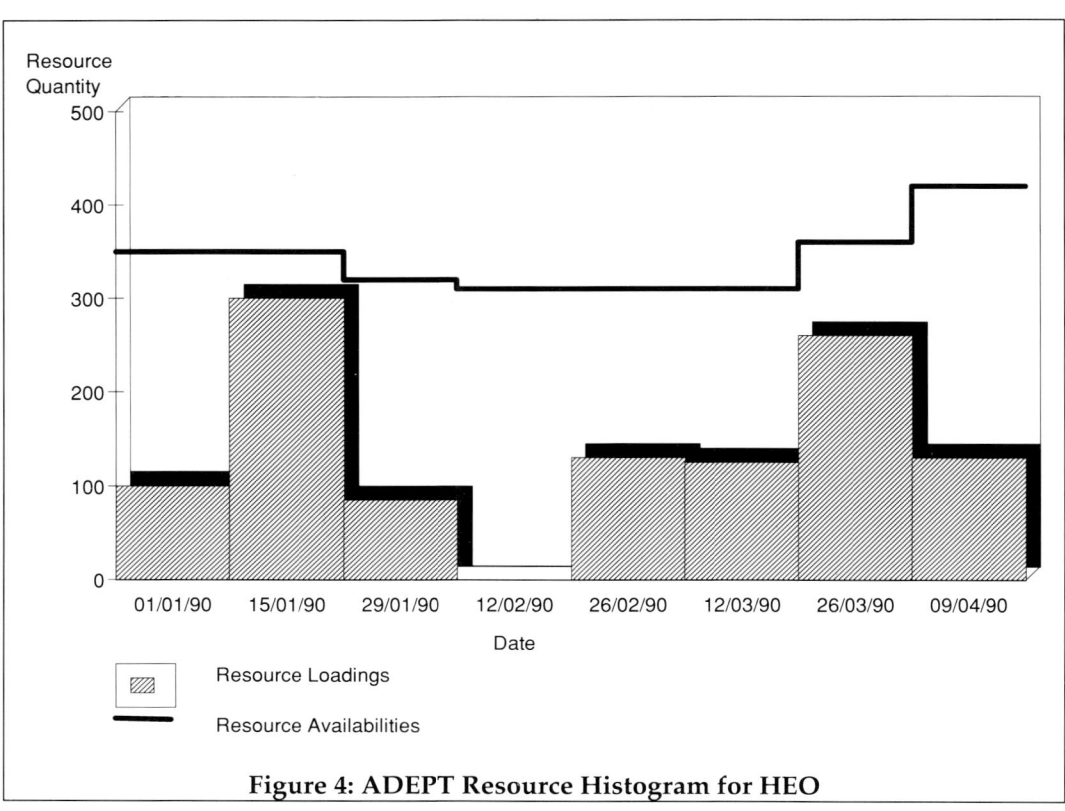

Figure 4: ADEPT Resource Histogram for HEO

Resource Histogram	A Resource Histogram, figure 4, shows a project's planned and actual resources against a timescale, enabling the project manager to monitor the expenditure of resources and to control over- and under-utilization. Over-resourcing has an obvious impact on the costs of a project. Under-resourcing may indicate a higher productivity than planned, or it may be a sign of corners being cut and a potential impact on quality.
Cost Graph	A Cost Graph, as shown in figure 5, allows comparisons between budget and expenditure to be made.
Checkpoint meetings	In a large project, communication between the numerous task groups is often limited, leading to a sense of isolation and demotivation in the teams. These problems can be overcome through the use of regular progress review meetings with the team leaders.

Section 3
Project management and liaison

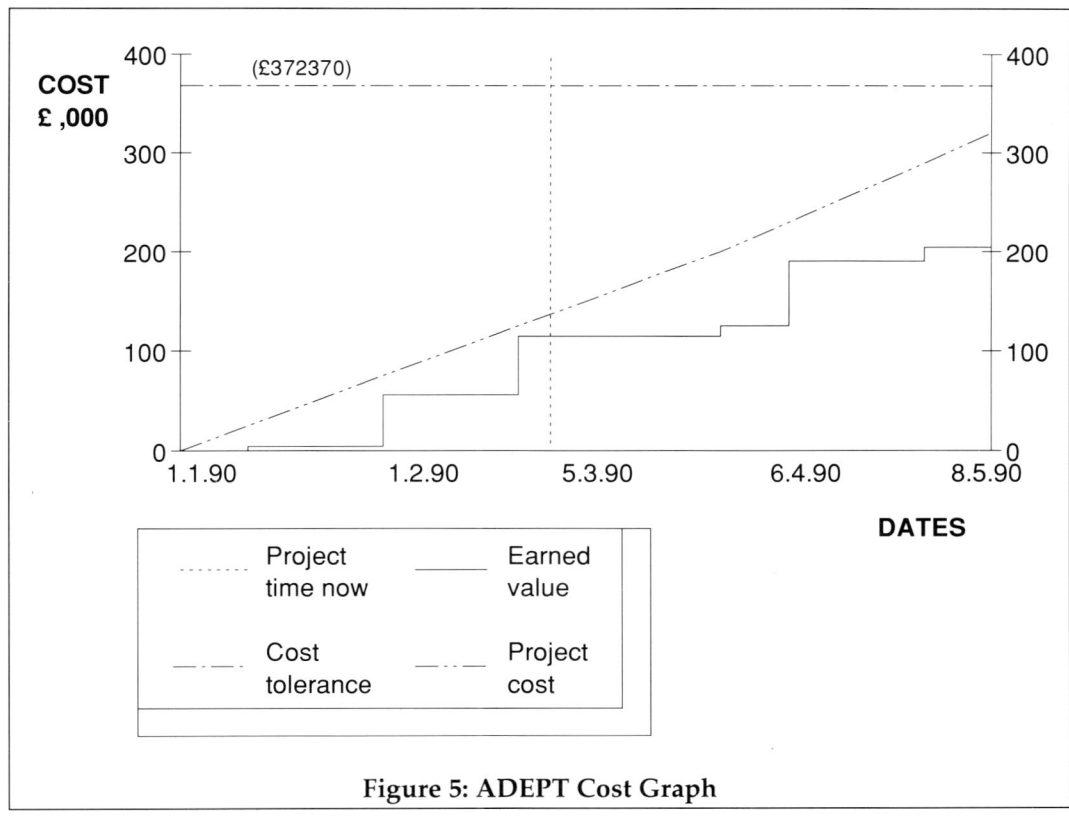

Figure 5: ADEPT Cost Graph

The benefits of these meetings, explained in the PRINCE manuals, are:

* liaison and communication between teams
* information flow to the project manager on progress, both to date and expected
* early warning of problems and conflicts, and a forum for their resolution.

To be effective, PRINCE recommends that these meetings be held on fixed dates, between once a week and once a month. They must have a formal agenda and be minuted.

Exception plans If a project needs to deviate, or shows signs of deviation from the plan, an exception plan will be required to explain the situation and request approval for corrective measures. The project manager may, for example, seek approval to increase resources to avoid a project overrun.

3.4 Contributors to the specification

To ensure that the cable infrastructure specification is correct, realistic and achievable, attention must be given to identifying and involving all the necessary contributors to the specification. So that time and resources are not wasted, it is essential that these sources are identified at the beginning of the specification process.

Typical contributors to an infrastructure specification are:

* Senior IS Managers
* IT staff, including the cabling manager
* budget managers
* users
* specialist external IT consultants
* architects
* accommodation officers
* mechanical and electrical engineering consultants.

User requirement survey

Although some contributors will be individuals, an important element of the specification task will be to determine the requirements and representation of groups, such as the users. Senior users, representing the business, will be able to contribute at a strategic level to the specification since they have direct access to the IT Executive Committee. However, it may be necessary to conduct a survey of end users to find out the initial requirements or to identify non-strategic applications that cannot be supported on the cable infrastructure. The effort needed to conduct a thorough user requirements survey is often significant, as many end users normally have little technical knowledge of their present requirements, and no long-term view of future requirements.

Matrix of responsibilities

On a major project, such as a cable infrastructure, it is likely that a number of contributors will have an input to each facet of the specification. It is also likely that a team consisting of specialists from a variety of work disciplines will be involved in producing the specification, each liaising with several contributors. To avoid conflicts, duplication of effort or overlooking the needs of any group, the project manager should compile a matrix of responsibilities, in format similar to that shown in figure 6.

Section 3
Project management and liaison

Contributor	Specifier			Work disciplines				
	Networks	Cable media	Quantification	Computer room spec.	Network room spec.	PABX room spec.	Risers	M & E
Department A user				●	O	O		
Department B user	●	O	O		O			
Department C user		O	O			●		
Architect				O	O	O	●	O
M & E consultant				O	O	O	O	●
IT consultant	●	O	O	O	O	O	O	O
Budget manager A				●				
Budget manager B	●							
Budget manager C						●		
Network manager (data)	●	O						
Network manager (voice)		O				●		
Standards officer	●							

Key: ● Major Responsibility   O General Responsibility

Figure 6: Project Team Responsibility Matrix

Each contributor is listed on the left, forming the rows of the matrix, and the work disciplines form the column headings. Open circles in a cell indicate that there is a requirement to be considered in the specification; closed circles indicate the major responsibilities. There must be one, but only one, work discipline - for example, M&E services - with major responsibility for the interests of each contributor.

From the matrix, contributors can clearly identify their own representative in the production of the specification, helping to maintain their motivation and interest in the project.

3.5 Influences of the IS strategy

By nature, corporate information systems are dynamic. They change with changing business requirements. The IT infrastructure, on which the corporate IT services are based, needs to be able to accommodate changes in both IT equipment and the IT services. Changing business needs demand an IT infrastructure which is flexible and adaptable.

Tactical planning for the provision of IT information systems is not confined to determining IT applications and IT services that may be required by the organization. The planning concentrates on providing an IT infrastructure which will support any IT service need the organization may have, or which can readily be enhanced to provide IT services as business evolves.

The cable infrastructure, carrying the information, is an integral part of the IT infrastructure. The IT infrastructure cannot function effectively without a suitable cable infrastructure. So it is essential to have a cable infrastructure which can support the changing demands to be placed upon it by evolving IT services.

The cable components of the IT infrastructure will be specified for a typical life of up to 15 years. During this life time several generations of IT services may be implemented. For example:

* penetration of workstations, increasing to one per desk

* comprehensive local area networking will be required to support pervasive use of IT

* high bandwidth transmissions, such as image processing, will influence choice of cable media

* voice recognition applications will bring technology changes and possible changes in data rate requirements and protocols.

The IS Strategy has a major influence in the specification of a cable infrastructure and its long term management requirements, and must be agreed before any cable infrastructure is specified.

3.6 Strategic constraints on the specification

The specification may be influenced by two strategic constraints - building strategy, and financial considerations.

Building strategy

Buildings may or may not be assets. A site will often be owned freehold by the organization or be on a long leasehold agreement. Other buildings may be subject to a short-term lease or rental agreement.

A well specified cable infrastructure will add value to a property. For freeholds or long leaseholds, this value may be realized by the organization when the site is sold or let. However, the investment made in short-term occupancy may be lost on expiry of the lease or termination of the rental agreement.

An additional implication of the building strategy is that short-term occupancy of a site restricts the payback period available for any investment made in strategic cabling.

The implications of the constraints that may be imposed by a particular building are discussed in Sections 9.7 and 9.8.

Financial considerations

Assuming that an organization is prepared to invest in its infrastructure strategy, four further constraints, three imposed by the internal financial strategy of an organization and one external, may influence the specification of a cable infrastructure:

* investment appraisal
* balance between capital and revenue expenditure
* strategy for cost recovery from users
* pressure on architects to maximize the net lettable area (NLA) of the building.

A cable infrastructure could have a typical useful life of up to 15 years - although investment, for example, in riser capacity, will give benefits for the life of the building. Strategic cabling should therefore be appraised over the same period as other building assets (eg building services) - typically 10 years. Unfortunately, many organizations look at only a much shorter period when evaluating an investment, particularly in the IT/IS environment. The business case for cabling may therefore be forced to focus on benefits accruing in the first three to five years, affecting the specification, for example, in the choice of cabling media.

Cable infrastructures require greater initial (capital) investment than ad-hoc cabling, but produce a greater saving in the operational (current) budgets. This is a key justification for considering an infrastructure strategy. Unfortunately, the true current costs of maintaining existing systems are rarely known since costs are often absorbed over a number of departmental budgets and cost centres. Quantification of the likely savings through the use of strategic cabling is therefore made difficult, and underestimation is likely. As a result, the investment appraisal for strategic cabling is weakened, constraining the options available to those with a low initial cost. These arguments are detailed in the IT Infrastructure Library module **Cable Infrastructure Strategy**.

Many, but not all, organizations have implemented systems to recover the costs of central IT/IS facilities from the users. Typically, this is applied to telephony, with a flat charge per extension in addition to any charges for calls made. The costs of cable infrastructure are harder to recover. For example, should a user pay for the connection provided to an office, even if it is not used, and what proportion of the capital investment should be recovered from the first users? The constraint on the specification is that users unused to paying realistic prices for IT may influence the specification to reduce initial costs to themselves, rather than considering longer-term corporate benefits.

Although there are encouraging signs of change, architects have been under pressure to maximize the lettable space of a development. Risers, which form part of the service core, are not included in the NLA of a building, and are therefore regarded as unprofitable space. The effect is visible in many buildings, where space for cables, plant rooms and communications closets is inadequate, and buildings are demolished because of their inability to support IT. Organizations financing or specifying building shells must be prepared to pay for IT accommodation, and to regard it as valuable space.

Despite these constraints, the potential financial benefits of strategic cabling can far outweigh the higher initial costs over tactical cabling. Not only are ongoing costs reduced, but the organization will also be able to respond effectively to new business opportunities and developments in technology - saving money and maximizing benefits.

Section 4
Cable infrastructure management

4. Cable infrastructure management

4.1 The cable infrastructure as an asset

Asset management is an essential aspect of any business. A cable infrastructure is a strategic IT asset, and must be managed as such if the organization's business is to be conducted effectively.

The objective of cable infrastructure management is to ensure that the benefits of investment in cabling are maintained over the life of the installation. Ongoing management is an essential component of a cable infrastructure project, and procedures and management tools must be planned as a part of the specification process.

Experience has shown that many cable infrastructures have failed to deliver the functionality expected, not through poor design, but because the management aspects were not given the necessary priority or support. Common reasons for organizations losing control of cabling are that management procedures have not been implemented in areas such as documentation, change control and security.

A cable infrastructure, like most other assets, will degenerate if it is not properly managed. Poor management is likely to result in inaccurate documentation, poor installation practices and a general lack of confidence in the cable infrastructure. For example, inadequate labelling may make it impossible to identify cables installed for resilience, and a failure to control access to the infrastructure may result in an unmanageable free-for-all as users try to configure the cabling for moves and changes or to move cables to new locations.

Once installation is completed, the cabling becomes a fundamental element of the IT infrastructure, and should be brought under change management. Many of the management issues are covered by their own IT Infrastructure Library modules, which are referenced later in this section.

4.2 Configuration management

Configuration management is a discipline, normally supported by software tools, that facilitates strict control of corporate IT assets by allowing the organization to:

* list each item in the infrastructure, with information on

    - the status of each item (for example, in live use, archived, scheduled for live use)

    - ownership of each item (the individual with prime responsibility for it)

    - the relationships between items

* maintain current records containing these pieces of information

* control changes by ensuring that they are made only with the agreement of authorized parties (see 4.3)

* audit the IT infrastructure to ensure that it corresponds exactly to the records.

The configuration management process within an organization may control hardware devices, software, documentation, corporate IT services, telecommunications services and the cable infrastructure.

Management of a cable infrastructure should be specified as an integral part of an organization's configuration management, and will ultimately be the responsibility of a Configuration Manager. A consistent documentation and labelling method for cabling and other IT elements should be specified to reduce the scope for confusion and errors.

Further guidance on this topic is available from the IT Infrastructure Library module **Configuration Management**.

4.3 Change control procedures

The versatility of a strategic cable infrastructure is provided by the ability to reconfigure the cross connects in the closets. These changes will be the repatching of connections to reconfigure the IT services as the building occupants move, rearrange their work areas or require different, additional, or fewer, services.

Section 4
Cable infrastructure management

If an infrastructure is not strategic, there may also be occasional requests for cables to be added or removed - for example, the installation of fibre-to-the-desk or of additional backbone cabling.

To manage these changes, two change control procedures must be specified to ensure that:

* changes are co-ordinated centrally, via the help desk, and that only authorized staff or contractors make changes to the infrastructure - and only at an agreed time

* a request for change (RFC) is generated, recorded and approved before a change is made. RFCs are used to maintain the configuration management records, and to generate work dockets for the change. Confirmation procedures should be used to verify that a requested change has been validated, and that the records have been updated.

Change control procedures should be specified as a series of steps, as illustrated in the example in figure 7, overleaf. However, it should be noted that the procedure for cable infrastructure changes must be the same as that agreed for the IT infrastructure as a whole. The specification of change control procedures for the cabling should not be taken in isolation.

The IT Infrastructure Library module **Change Management** will guide the reader in the implementation of change control procedures.

4.4 Use of the help desk

A help desk will form the main day-to-day interface between the providers and users of the services delivered over the IT infrastructure.

The cable infrastructure should not be managed in isolation from other aspects of the IT infrastructure; users should have a single point of contact with the IT support functions for desk-top equipment and cabling. Duplication of the support service will lead to inefficiencies and confusion on both sides of the help desk.

Guidance on creating and successfully operating a user help desk function is available from the IT Infrastructure Library module **Help Desk**.

The IT Infrastructure Library
Specification and Management of a Cable Infrastructure

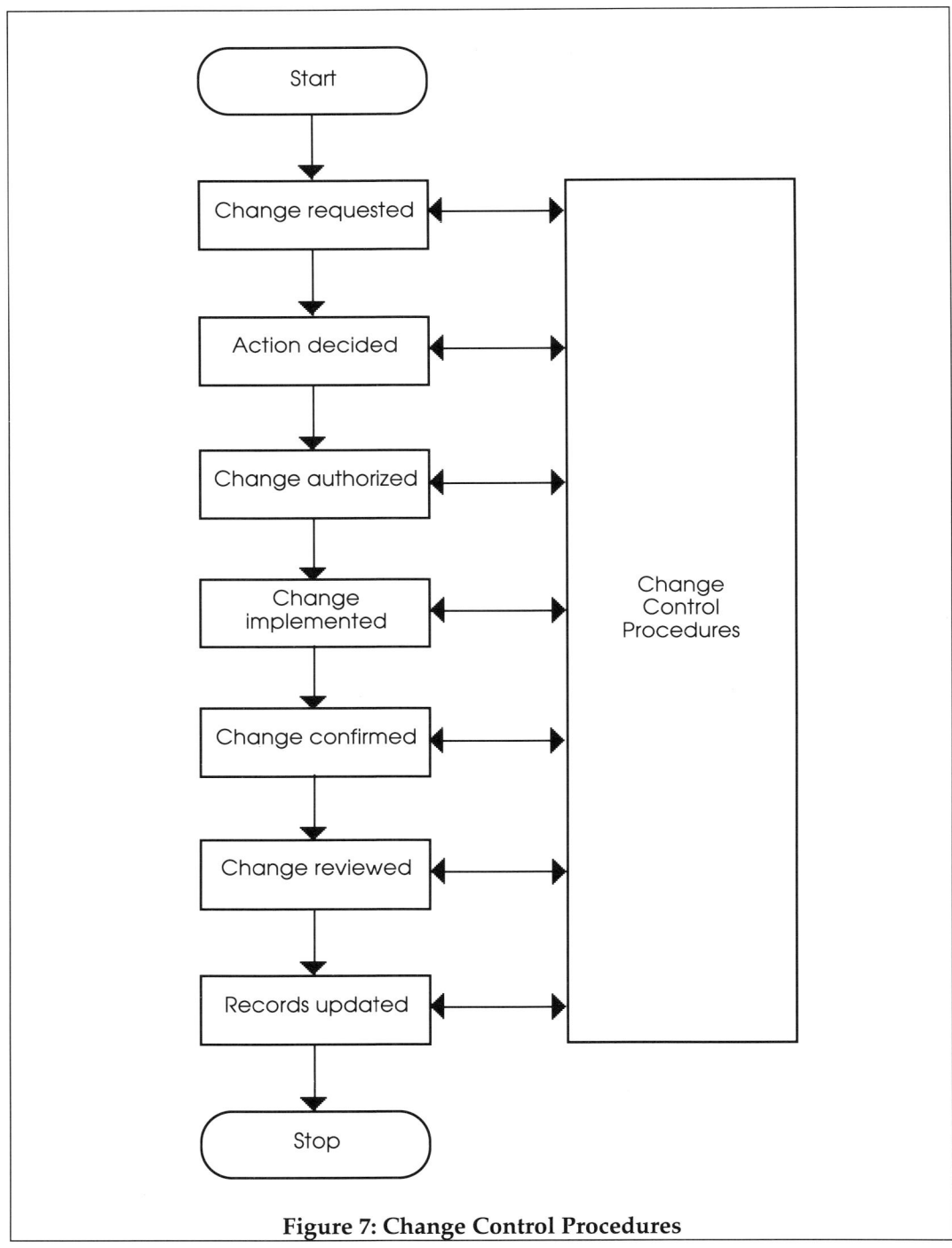

Figure 7: Change Control Procedures

Section 4
Cable infrastructure management

4.5 Auditing

Audit requirements and procedures may need to be included in the specification of an infrastructure.

The IT Services Manager should consider authorizing an audit of an existing cable installation if:

* it is necessary to remove obsolete cables selectively as part of an upgrade or phased infrastructure implementation. (The objective of the audit is to identify surplus cables so that they can be removed without disrupting live services.)

* records are known to be inaccurate or there are doubts about their accuracy. (The audit serves to establish the formal records necessary for ongoing management.)

* periodic, often annual, checks are required to confirm that the records are correct.

Where accurate records have been established, and when resources do not permit a full audit, periodic audits should be done on a sampling basis, typically of 10 per cent. However, if the sample shows the records to contain inaccuracies, a full audit must be carried out.

For an audit to be possible, the components of the IT infrastructure must all be clearly identifiable. Further information on auditing is available from the IT Infrastructure Library module **Quality Management for IT Services**.

4.6 Component identification

For effective configuration management, it is essential that all the components within the infrastructure are identified. For the use of computerized records, unique identification of each item is essential. To be effective, the identification method must be:

* specified at the outset of an infrastructure project

* common to all elements (for example, cables, electronics, connections)

* included in all contracts with suppliers and maintainers

* rigorously enforced.

The IT Infrastructure Library
Specification and Management of a Cable Infrastructure

To enable components to be identified quickly, and to reduce the scope for errors, the identification scheme specified should give an indication of the service, type, vendor (or maintainer), and the end equipment (to user or connection level) for a cable or piece of equipment.

For the required information to be presented clearly, the identification will typically consist of a number of alpha-numeric fields as illustrated in the example, figure 8.

Equipment identification format: A-AA-A-NNNN

Cable identification format: A-AA-A-NNNN

Key:

Field	Information	Format	Examples
A	Responsibility	A-Z	B=BT M=Mercury
AA	service	AA-ZZ	NS=network services
A	type	A-Z	M=modem C=coax
NNNN	unique number	0001-9999	

Connection identification format: AA-nnn-A-NNN-n

Key:

Field	Information	Format	Examples
AA	building	AA-ZZ	HO=head office
nnn	floor	free	001, -2, GND
A	closet	A-Z	B=second closet on floor nnn
NNN	presentation	001-999	123=123rd presentation
n	connection	free	1=voice, 2=data

Figure 8: Example component identification method

Section 4
Cable infrastructure management

Labelling

Specifying the labelling of equipment, frames and patch fields is normally straightforward: a clear label is required on each item and by each connection. However, specifying the labelling of cables is not so straightforward. The ideal is to be able to identify every cable anywhere along its length, so that it can be identified at the location of any damage. However, labelling this frequently is time-consuming and the organization must assess the benefit of quick incident location against the additional cost. A recommended compromise is to label cables at the following points:

* every 5 metres along the length
* at each entry point to a riser
* at each exit from a riser
* at any bend of 90 degrees or more
* on each side of a wall, sleeve or fire break.

An example of a cable labelling method that might be included in a requirement specification is shown in figure 9, overleaf.

It is important that labelling is carried out during installation and not implemented retrospectively. This is to remove the problems of, for example, labelling a cable once it is buried under others in a tray or tied into the back of a cabinet. Regular checks, on a daily basis if required, should be made, by a representative of the procuring organization, of contractors' work to ensure that the labelling specification is being followed. To ensure compliance, the organization should consider specifying the right to have cut out any non-conforming cable - to be replaced by the contractor at no additional charge.

4.7 Incident reporting and logging

Incident reporting and logging procedures should be based on the problem management procedures, and be co-ordinated from the IT help desk. In addition to the functions of problem management, the incident management procedures must also be specified to include the formal recording of reliability, availability and serviceability (RAS) information.

RAS records indicate the number and type of incidents occurring, and enable a comparison to be made between availability levels achieved and those specified in the

The IT Infrastructure Library
Specification and Management of a Cable Infrastructure

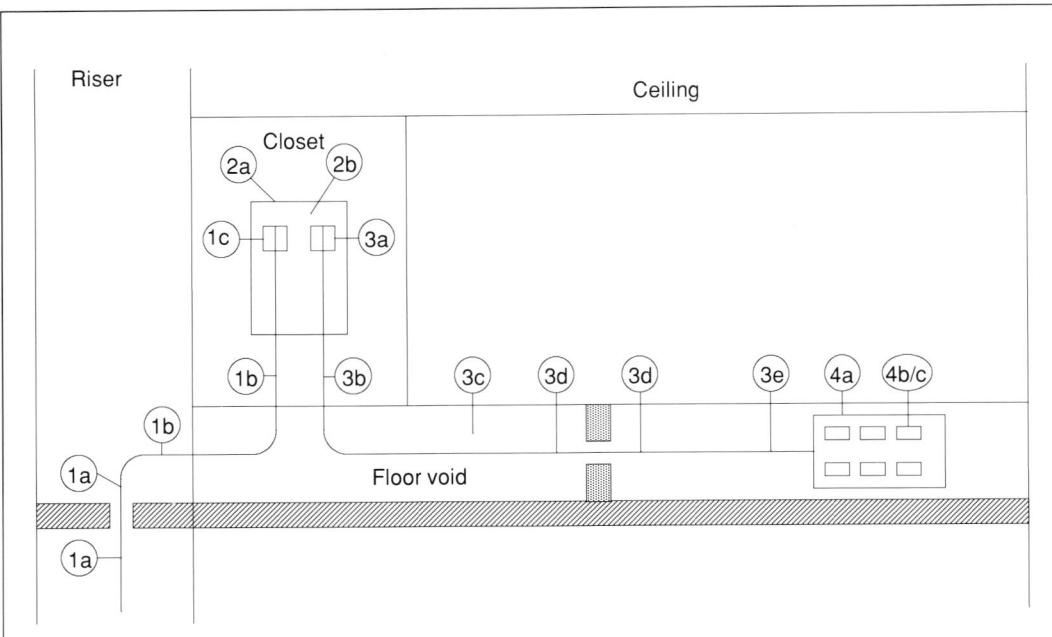

Item	Description	Labels	Type
1	Riser cable	a) Both sides of fire barrier b) Both sides of entry c) On terminal designation strips	Proprietary cable label Proprietary cable label Indelible pen
2	Termination panel	a) On outside cover b) Inside	Indelible marker Indelible marker
3	Horizontal cable	a) On terminal designation strips b) Inside closet c) Every 5 metres d) Both sides of fire barrier e) Where cable leaves basket	Indelible pen Proprietary cable label Proprietary cable label Proprietary cable label Proprietary cable label
4	Underfloor connection point	a) On cover b) On front of socket c) On rear of socket	Indelible marker Engraved plastic label Indelible marker

Figure 9: Cable labelling requirements

service level agreements. This comparison also enables the organization to monitor and manage its maintenance contracts by comparing product serviceability with the conditions of the maintenance contract.

The procedure for problem management within the cable infrastructure must be in accordance with that used for the IT infrastructure as a whole, and consists of a series of steps similar to those illustrated in figure 10. The incident reporting procedures, together with the types of report to be used, should be included in the maintenance contract for the cable infrastructure.

Guidance on the collection and use of RAS information is available from the IT Infrastructure Library module **Problem Management**.

4.8 Maintenance

Maintenance of a cable infrastructure should be planned, specified and managed as an integral part of the IT infrastructure management, and not carried out in isolation. The maintenance requirements must be determined by the overall availability requirement of the services supported by the infrastructure, and specified early enough to ensure that maintainability is designed into the infrastructure.

It is important that maintenance provision is carefully matched to the business requirements, and not over-specified. Over-specification will result in unnecessary resilience being procured and excessive maintenance charges.

Examples of typical maintenance-cover requirements are included in Section 5.

Contracts

The maintenance contract should reflect the user service level requirements, which are discussed in Section 5. The specifier of an infrastructure for a government installation is recommended to follow the CCTA's Rules for Tendering and General Conditions of Contract, CC88. Part 2-C covers the provision of maintenance services.

Tools

Most tools and techniques required for the management of a cable infrastructure are the same as those used for tactical cabling of voice and data. They include:

* network management tools to monitor live data traffic

* bit error rate testers to simulate data traffic and monitor data corruption during commissioning

* breakout boxes used to check interface compatibility.

The IT Infrastructure Library
Specification and Management of a Cable Infrastructure

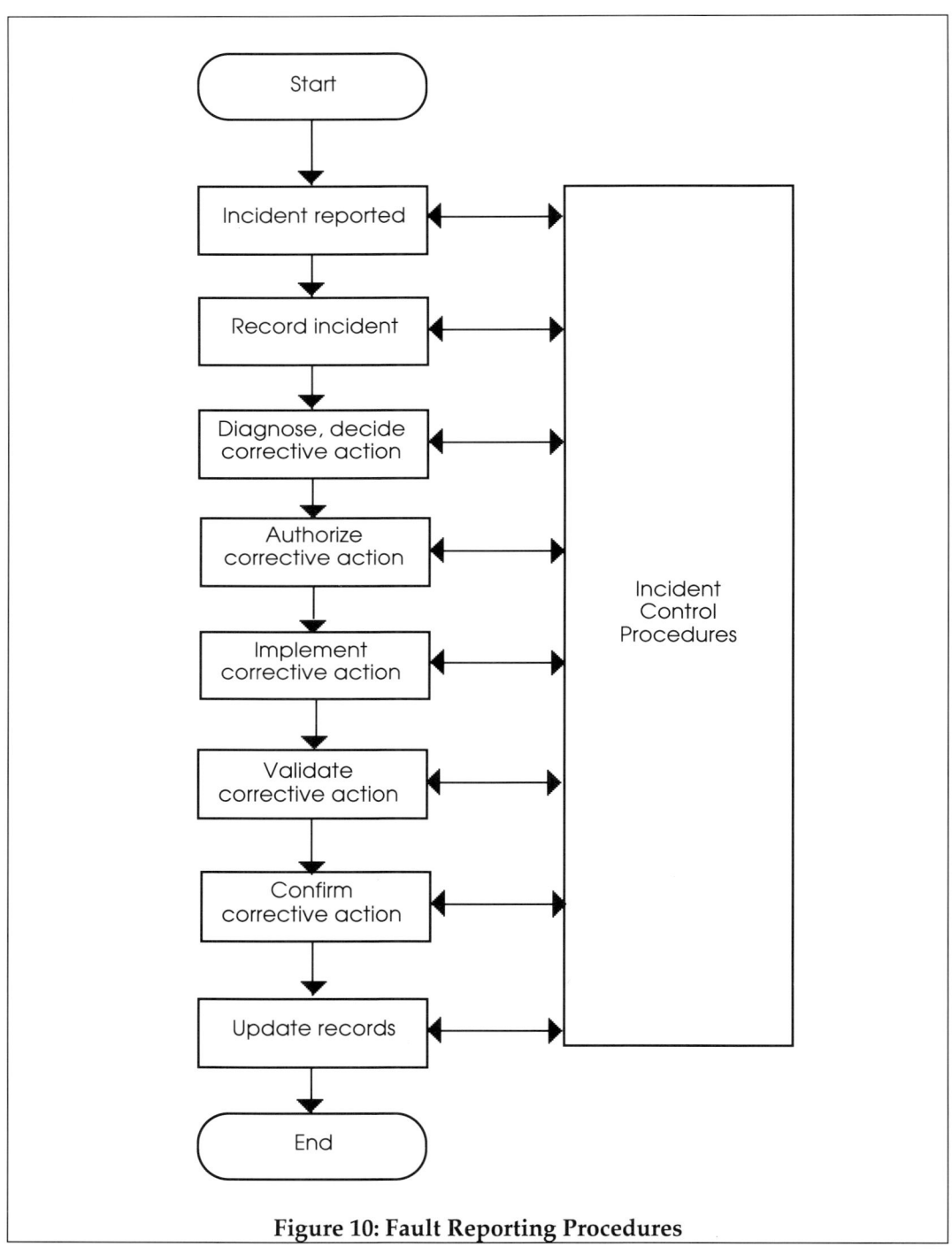

Figure 10: Fault Reporting Procedures

Section 4
Cable infrastructure management

For fibre-optic testing, many of the tools are derived from familiar copper-based test sets, although some, such as the optical time domain reflectometer (OTDR) used for incident location and attenuation measurements, are more complex and require specialist training if the user is to obtain the maximum benefit from their use.

One extra tool that is essential for strategic cabling and not used in tactical implementations is a cable management package. This could be paper-based, but it is recommended that a software package is specified for greater flexibility and the additional features that it can offer. A number of cable management products are available, and help in choosing a suitable product is given in Section 16, Cable management tools.

4.9 Managing cables carrying sensitive data

The management of secure cables poses a particular problem in a cable infrastructure because of the threat of intercepts on communications at the cross connects and patch fields, as well as by tapping into the cables directly. A further potential problem is that all cables in the infrastructure should be readily identifiable along their length.

Unlabelled cables are not recommended because they undermine infrastructure management, by nature of being unlabelled they are conspicuous. An overlay of cables could be used, avoiding the management issues, but again this is not a strategic solution.

It is therefore recommended that cables carrying secure traffic are managed as a part of the infrastructure, but that special care is given to controlling access to the cabling elements, and that the labelling is chosen to prevent identification of the traffic being carried.

For maximum security, cable routes (not the cables) should be visible so that any physical interference can readily be detected.

The use of fibre-optic cables is often recommended when data security is important. Unlike copper cables, fibre-optics do not generate radiation susceptible to passive electronic eavesdropping. Although fibre can be tapped, it is an intrusive operation and, with appropriate expertise, it is possible to detect the resulting loss of light and locate the intrusion.

4.10 Recording logical and physical relationships

A strategic cable infrastructure will usually be installed as a star topology, as shown in figure 15 (p54). However, this physical relationship does not constrain the infrastructure to supporting only logical star configurations. The nature of the interconnections and adapters in the cross connects and telecommunications closets also allows for bus, ring, and tree configurations. These configurations are shown in figures 17, 18 and 19 (pp57-60).

The cable management tool specified must be capable of indicating the physical connections between any two points on the infrastructure. The route could be shown as a schematic diagram, as a highlighted path on a drawing, or as a list of component identifications. What it may not be able to show are the logical relationships - for example, which users are connected to the same bus or ring. Although software is being developed that will be able to record both physical and logical relationships, it is not generally available at the time of writing and it may be necessary for the organization to maintain a separate record of logical relationships by use of a Configuration Management tool.

Cable management records should be maintained by the configuration management authority, and the production of records should be included in the requirements specification. If the logical topology is specified as a part of the installation contract, then the requirements for both physical and logical documentation should be included in the OR.

4.11 Resilience and contingency measures

Resilience and contingency must be provided to maintain or restore the availability of service to the users in the event of IT service delivery failures, and their planning is a part of the infrastructure management.

The resilience specified as a part of the infrastructure - for example, through the use of dual cable routes - is provided to maintain the service levels during component failures and some disaster situations.

Contingency measures are implemented only when the resilience in the infrastructure is unable to maintain acceptable service to the users. Examples of contingency measures would be:

* plans to relocate key parts of the business to alternative premises

* a contract to provide a replacement computer suite in the event of a major disaster

* provision of a command room with access to voice and data services to act as a control centre under emergency situations.

The level of contingency planning required will be determined by the balance between the cost of failing to provide IT services against the cost of making the contingency provision, allowing for the degree of risk that the organization is prepared to accept. This balancing is known as risk analysis.

The specification of a cable infrastructure must include resilience requirements, and the specifier should also co-ordinate the specification with the central contingency plans of the organization. It is also important that the provisions for resilience and contingency be reviewed regularly - for example, on an annual basis - to ensure that they still meet fully the needs of the organization. The vulnerability of any cables that pass through high-risk, hazardous areas should be given careful consideration when the risks are being assessed.

4.12 Resources

Resource costs will be incurred since cable management systems must be operated, the help desk supported and cable audits conducted. The contingency measures adopted will have an associated cost, even if they are never actually used. However, management of the cable infrastructure is vital if the benefits from taking a strategic approach are to be realized, and the organization must be prepared to make the investment required, both initially and during the life of the infrastructure. The resources required will be determined by the size of the infrastructure, the practices of the organization and the tools deployed.

The IT Infrastructure Library
Specification and Management of a Cable Infrastructure

Section 5
Reliability and resilience

5. Reliability and resilience

5.1 The importance of availability

User expectation — Users of IT expect to have quality services delivered to the desk, and available when needed, to enable them to work effectively. As many organizations are dependent on IT to carry out business, the consequences of delivery failure become more serious. When any part of the IT infrastructure is being specified, these business and user requirements must be formally agreed between the users and the providers of the IT service.

Availability — An IT infrastructure includes cabling. It is therefore essential that the operational quality of the cable infrastructure fully complements and underpins the user requirements for quality of IT services delivery. For a cable infrastructure, one aspect of quality is availability - that is, the percentage of time that the IT services it supports are available to the users.

Service Level Agreement — A Service Level Agreement (SLA) is recommended by CCTA as the best way of agreeing on requirements, and formalizing an arrangement between the IT service providers and the service users for the availability of IT services. The IT systems delivering these services are supported by suppliers and maintainers. Contracts with these bodies must be based on the SLAs whenever possible. Each maintenance contract is subject to its own contractual minimum serviceability, and the SLA must be able to cater for each of them being a 'worst case' level during the monitoring period. This hierarchy, with the users at the top, is shown in figure 11, overleaf.

The cost of availability — The specifier of the infrastructure must ensure that the users are expressing real needs, and not ideal wants, before agreeing to the users' availability requests. The steps to be taken are to assess the financial costs of meeting users' stated availability requirements, and present them to the users managers for approval. If the costs of providing the desired availability outweigh the benefits to the business, the process will have to be repeated until the costs and benefits of an availability level are acceptable to both parties.

IT service availability — As well as the serviceability and reliability of IT equipment, covered by maintenance contract conditions (discussed above), availability of an IT service at the user desk will be influenced by other factors. Among these other factors will be the environmental infrastructure, including the cabling.

The IT Infrastructure Library
Specification and Management of a Cable Infrastructure

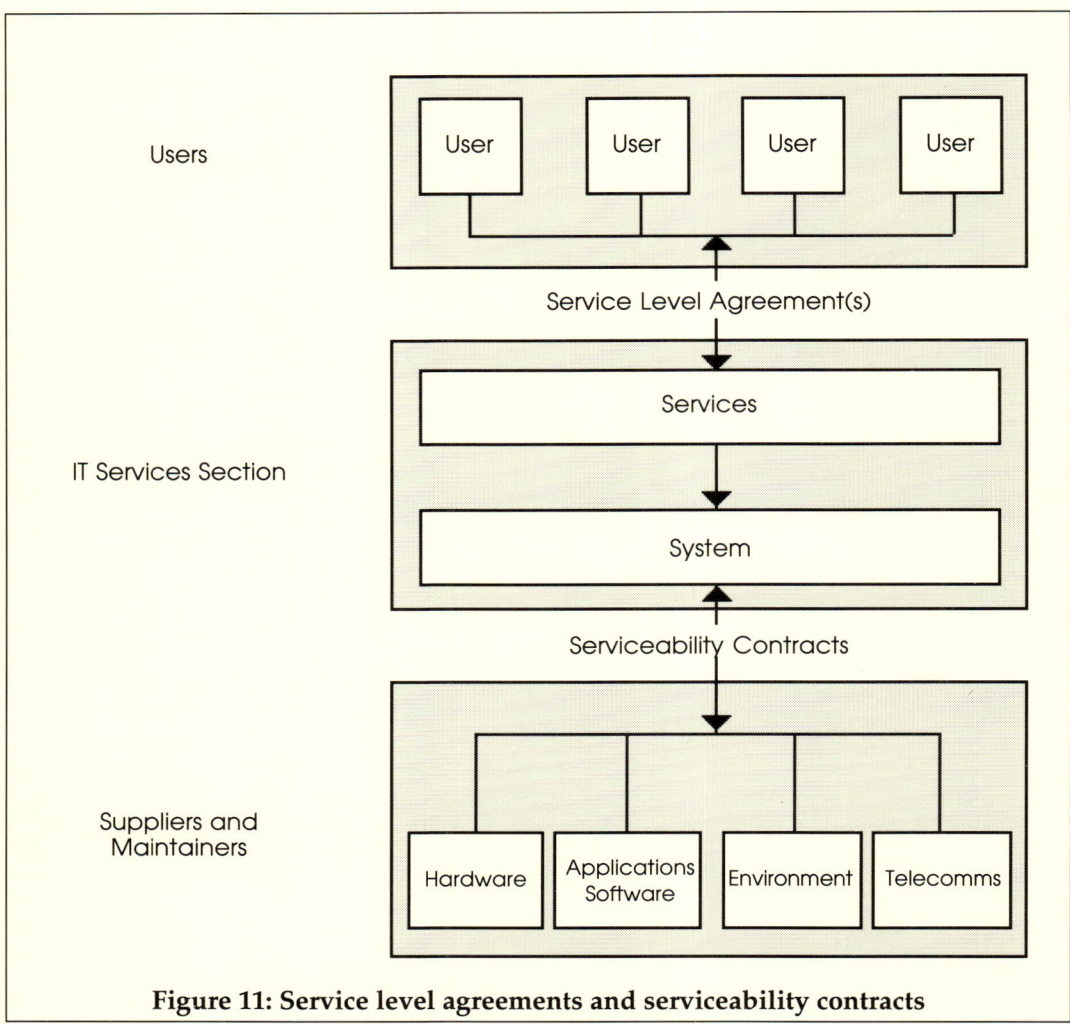

Figure 11: Service level agreements and serviceability contracts

Factors influencing availability

For non-critical applications, the simplest cable infrastructure may be sufficiently reliable to meet the quality requirements of users. For others, high resilience will have to be specified. The vast majority of applications will fall between these two extremes.

The ability of a cable infrastructure to deliver IT services to the users is determined by five main factors:

* quality of the design and installation

* reliability of the components that make up the infrastructure

Section 5
Reliability and resilience

* vulnerability to external factors, such as fire, flood, accident or sabotage
* resilience of the infrastructure to failures
* speed with which failures can be rectified.

Further guidance on availability can be obtained from the IT Infrastructure Library modules **Service Level Management** and **Availability Management**.

5.2 Quality and availability requirements

MTBF/MTBR

Theoretical downtime, or unserviceability, can be calculated from mean time between failures (MTBF) and mean time to repair (MTTR) figures. The latter are available either empirically, from the vendors' or maintainers' specifications, or from the conditions imposed in a maintenance contract. However, it must be borne in mind that MTBF figures exclude the unexpected events originating from outside the infrastructure, which can also lead to a loss of service, such as the pick axe through an underground cable, power failures, or a fire in a riser.

Contingency planning

Planning is required to identify possible disasters, their probability, and their impact on the infrastructure's ability to deliver IT services to the users. The levels of risk that an organization is prepared to accept, and the cost of providing protection, will determine the degree of resilience specified in the infrastructure. Full contingency planning is beyond the scope of this module.

Common availability

The organization must take a long-term view when deciding whether or not to specify a common availability level throughout the infrastructure. From a strategic point of view, a common level of availability is sensible, as it prevents any constraints being placed on the location of staff and services throughout the building. However, as this common level must meet the requirements of the most demanding services, it may stretch the financial budget unacceptably, and a carefully considered compromise may be necessary. Financial constraints should not, however, be allowed to compromise a structured approach. The organization must also decide how the availability requirements of the infrastructure will change during its life and specify availability levels based on future requirements.

The IT Infrastructure Library
Specification and Management of a Cable Infrastructure

5.3 Specifying for reliability and resilience

5.3.1 Why specify reliability and resilience?

The specifier must be able to present the requirements imposed by the SLAs to suppliers and maintainers. The specifier, through the Operational Requirement (OR), must also indicate how serviceability is to be calculated. Guidance in these areas is to be found in CC88, CCTA's Rules for Tendering and General Conditions of Contract. When evaluating responses, the specifier should be aware of how availability can be calculated, and of the other, external, factors to be considered.

5.3.2 Reliability

Determining reliability

Reliability is a measure of how often an item fails to function. The usual way of quantifying reliability is the measure of MTBF. A system's reliability is determined by the reliability of its individual components, and by the number of components that must operate to provide the service.

An IT infrastructure, as a system, could include heating, ventilation and air conditioning (HVAC), power and computing equipment. The failure of any one of these subsystems to operate could lead to a total system failure. The specifier must realize that the subsystems are not independent, and must plan overall system reliability accordingly.

Enhancing reliability

Steps that can be taken to enhance the reliability of a cable infrastructure are to specify quality products with high serviceability and to reduce the number of points of failure by avoiding unnecessary system complexity. In addition, thorough quality control procedures during commissioning and acceptance testing (discussed further in Section 13) should be adopted to identify and replace any rogue elements in the infrastructure.

Reliability can also be improved by careful design of the infrastructure. For example, cooling to ensure that electronics operate within specification will slow component aging and increase the MTBF.

Quantifying reliability

Reliability can be derived either from field trials or from theoretical calculations based on the reliability of individual components. The reliability of cables is usually very good,

Section 5
Reliability and resilience

since there are no active parts to fail. The weak link in a cable infrastructure is usually the associated electronics for interfaces and networking. The figures quoted by equipment vendors for their products can be used to calculate an overall system MTBF, indicating the theoretical frequency of failures caused by component failures or software faults to be expected during normal operation.

5.3.3 Resilience

Importance

The level of resilience in a cable infrastructure determines the effect of the failure of one or more components on the delivery of IT services to the users. The greater the resilience, the less marked the effect. Although a very high level of resilience could be designed into a communication infrastructure to create a 'fail safe' installation, the cost should be contained by matching resilience to the service quality requirements of the organization.

The requirements and alternatives available for cabling are considered below.

Resilience and power

Specification of resilience for power supplies in an infrastructure is important. Section 10, Provision of environmental services, addresses the options of standby generators and uninterruptible power supplies.

Options for resilience

Resilience is often easier to specify than reliability, and provides a second level of protection for users through parallel elements or subsystems. There are a number of ways of designing resilience into a cable infrastructure. High availability in the event of a failure or disaster could be created by the use of redundant (duplicated) elements in the system. For example, users able to access a central service via two risers could still operate normally in the event of a fire destroying the cables in either riser. The provision of standby power generation for use when the grid power fails is another common example. However, duplication is expensive, and may not always be cost-justifiable.

If it is not essential to maintain service to all users in the event of a disaster, resilience can be provided without the need for redundancy, and with a considerable cost saving. For example, half the users in a department would have connections from one riser and the other half would have connections from another riser. In the event of a riser fire, half of the users could continue to work normally, or all of the users could manage by sharing terminals with a neighbour. This degradation in performance is often more acceptable than the costs of redundant components.

The IT Infrastructure Library
Specification and Management of a Cable Infrastructure

Diverse routeing The common cabling concept in the previous examples is diverse routeing also called multiple routeing. This method of routeing ensures that there are at least two independent ways of connecting a service to a user. Patching is used to configure the connections over an available route as required.

Ways of providing resilience Resilience can be provided in several ways. For example by:

* ensuring that each floor or work group is cabled from two or more risers and telecommunications closets

* interleaving connections to users from multiple closets on a floor

* installing spare cables so that connections can be restored without waiting for a damaged cable to be repaired or replaced

* distributing the cables for each service between risers

* connecting IT equipment, such as terminal servers, so that not all members of a group of users are dependent on the same unit

* splitting local area networks into smaller sections linked by bridges or gateways so that a faulty section can be isolated from the remainder (known as partitioning).

The supplier should select appropriate provisions to meet the availability levels specified in the Operational Requirement.

5.4 Maintenance

Maintenance provision should be considered as an integral part of the infrastructure, since it affects availability. The following guidelines are provided to help a cable infrastructure specifier define a maintenance requirement. Guidance on **Problem Management** is contained in the IT Infrastructure Library module of that name.

Use a help desk The Cabling Manager, who controls reconfiguration, must be the point of contact, via the help desk, in the event of a failure. The help desk should determine the cause of the delivery failure, record the fault and take appropriate remedial action. To ensure that the infrastructure management procedures are observed, and to avoid call-out charges for unnecessary work, users must not be permitted to attempt their own reconfiguration or to call out the maintenance organization.

Section 5
Reliability and resilience

Specify downtime
The organization should specify or designate the maximum allowable time to restore the service of each cabling element after a failure, and should make this a contractual obligation on the maintainer. No single response or repair time need be specified, since it is downtime that is important. The specified acceptable downtime need not be common for all elements. Typically, the vertical distribution will need to be returned to service faster than the horizontal elements since the impact of a backbone failure is more severe.

Maximum downtime
The downtime requirement should be specified by the use of maximum permitted downtime for incidents (Max DI). Figure 12 illustrates how this could be specified. The actual requirements will be determined by the existing SLAs or requirements of future services.

Figure 12: Maximum downtime for incidents

Incident	Typical maximum allowable downtime (working hours)
Loss of service to one user	8
Loss of service to 2-10 users	6
Loss of service to 11-50 users	4
Loss of service to over 50 users	2

Consider reliability
Although it is downtime that determines availability, reliability should also be considered. A large number of short failures may be more disruptive to the users than a few long failures - even if the total downtime is the same. CC88 includes guidance on specifying availability and reliability.

In-house maintenance
First-line reactive maintenance of cabling is often simply a matter of patching onto a redundant circuit or replacing a component, and it may be possible to do this quickly using an in-house resource, grouping tasks, and thereby saving costs. An organization keeping an on-site supply of cheap but regularly used components, such as patch leads and connectors, and carrying out first-line reactive maintenance, could expect to halve the cost of an annual maintenance contract for the cable installation, while maintaining the SLA and Max DIs specified. However, an organization should not attempt internal maintenance unless it has the skilled staff required, and support from the equipment vendors and second-line maintainers.

Rules

CCTA has produced a set of rules for tendering and general conditions for government contracts (CC88). These include guidance on the specification of maintenance provision appropriate to cable infrastructures.

5.5 Costs and benefits of reliability and resilience

Why invest?

For most organizations, the reason for investing in reliability and resilience is the cost to the business of interruptions in, or loss of, IT services (although the effect on staff morale of unreliable service may also be taken into account). The balancing constraints on the specification are the limits on the investment that an organization is prepared to make, the accommodation available in the building, and the degree of risk that the organization is prepared to accept.

A compromise is needed

The organization must make a compromise between these factors to match the quality of the infrastructure to the real needs of the business, and at a cost that the organization is prepared to pay. For example, backbone cabling may be dual-routed to prevent the loss of entire floors from a riser fire, while service to individual users is not protected by duplication.

Further costs

In addition to the initial costs of resilience, there will be associated ongoing costs. These will include management of a cable database and maintenance contracts. Over-specification of resilience will increase these costs unnecessarily - a factor to be considered when balancing requirements and costs.

6. Quantification

6.1 Quantification has become important

Definitions

Quantification is the calculation of the number of connections, presentations and cable media (cable types) required for voice, data and power by the users of a cable infrastructure. In more common terminology, connections can be visualized as sockets, and presentations (for example floor boxes) as outlets. A practical example is the domestic 13-amp twin socket outlet, which in IT infrastructure terminology, is a single presentation with two power connections.

Use of terms - a caution

The terms connection and presentation may appear contrived to the reader, and an unnecessary complication. Unfortunately, many of the terms in common usage have become ambiguous and are best avoided. For example, the term 'outlet' has been variously interpreted as a connection, a multiple connection, or an entire presentation. It is therefore vital that, for clear understanding, the project team agrees and applies a set of terms rigorously throughout the project.

Why the need for quantification?

In the past, a formal quantification method has seldom been used. The number of connections has been equal to the anticipated number of staff occupying a building, and the provision of one connection to each planned desk location has been considered adequate. Although this approach has worked for telephone wiring, experience shows that it is no longer valid with the recent changes, such as expansion of voice and data communications and the requirements for flexible office layouts. The result of these changes is usually a continual stream of requests from the building's occupants for connections to be moved or added, resulting in tactical cabling permeating the building. Obviating the need for these changes is the basic argument for strategic cabling, expounded in the IT Infrastructure Library module **Cable Infrastructure Strategy**.

6.2 Objectives

Objective of strategic cabling

As the key objective of strategic cabling is to eliminate tactical cabling, a cable infrastructure must be specified to satisfy the changing requirements of an organization's IT services without the need for recabling. The period required where there is no need for recabling could be as long as 15 years. To achieve the objective, there must always be enough connections, of the right type, in the right places, and at the right time, for the building occupants.

Objectives of quantification

The objectives of quantification are to:

* indicate the optimum number of connections
* indicate the optimum number of cable media
* indicate the density of presentations and number and types of connections for each.
* provide an effective method of distributing the connections to the users.

6.3 Connection quantification

Known or unknown occupancy

Knowing the occupancy of a building makes less difference than it may at first seems. Strategic cabling aims to support LANs conforming to standards and guidelines such as GOSIP. In general, it is not a tenable assumption that the requirements of occupants will remain static for the lifetime of a cable infrastructure. To provide connections on such a basis would assume that, over the life of the infrastructure:

* staff will not require a second terminal or telephone
* the number of staff will not increase
* all the connections will be within reach of the users, who will not wish to change the layout of the offices.

Experience has shown that few organizations could confidently make these predictions, and so this approach cannot be recommended as a quantification technique. The recommended approach is to plan connections and presentations as if the number of occupants were unknown.

If the number of occupants of the building is unknown, or cannot accurately be predicted over the lifespan of the infrastructure, then saturation wiring is recommended.

Saturated wiring

Saturation wiring is the planned and managed installation of many more connections than the number of users envisaged. Connections are provided to give full flexibility, even at the maximum possible user density, and distributed on a grid matrix throughout the building. Although only a proportion of the connections will be used at any one time, all are required to provide flexibility of office layout and meet the evolving requirements of the users, such as those requiring more than one service.

The **Cable Infrastructure Strategy** module states that a density for voice and data connections of one per four square metres of Net Lettable Area (NLA) of the building is often considered ideal. The number of voice and data connections required in a building can therefore be estimated quickly as the NLA of the building divided by four.

In practice, the estimate of connections can often be refined by subtracting from the NLA of the building, any areas that will not accommodate IT users. These reductions would include canteens and restaurants, communications closets, and primary circulation areas. It is not recommended that secondary circulation areas are deducted, since these may change during the lifetime of the infrastructure. The specifier must not scale down other infrastructure aspects such as risers or M & E services because other areas, such as restaurant areas, for example, may be converted to offices during the life of the building.

The number of power connections installed should be greater than the number for voice or data to avoid the need for multi-way adaptors or trailing power leads. Experience indicates that there must be two, and preferably three, power connections per presentation. For example, a work area may require a terminal, a task light and one other mains-powered device such as a printer, calculator, featurephone or answering machine.

6.4 Media quantification

The IS strategy of an organization will detail the expected future services and communications requirements in terms of strategic network standards and the associated data rates, traffic volumes, and implementation timescales.

Media quantification is the selection of the types of media required for the cable infrastructure. The media selection process will be based on the IS strategy. For example, if the IS strategy includes provision of high bandwidth services such as still or moving image or high-resolution graphics, then the use of fibre optics for vertical and horizontal cabling would be appropriate. However, should the strategic networks require LAN data rates only up to 10 or 16 million bits per second for the life-span of the infrastructure, then cheaper twisted pair cable could be more appropriate.

Unfortunately, some strategies neither contain sufficient detail nor extend far enough into the future to enable decisions on media types to be made with confidence. Experience has also shown that growths in data rates and bandwidth often significantly exceed even the most generous forecast. The solution, to avoid recabling, is to specify a cable infrastructure that includes a variety of cable media - for example, a copper distribution with provisions made for fibre to deliver the future high bandwidth services by including unterminated fibres or blown fibre ducting in the horizontal distribution, and presentations designed to accommodate optical connections. This mixed media solution is termed a hybrid cable infrastructure.

The adoption of standards will usually limit the choice of media. For example, by referencing EIA/TIA SP-1907 the media choices are narrowed down considerably since only a subset of all possible cables is included.

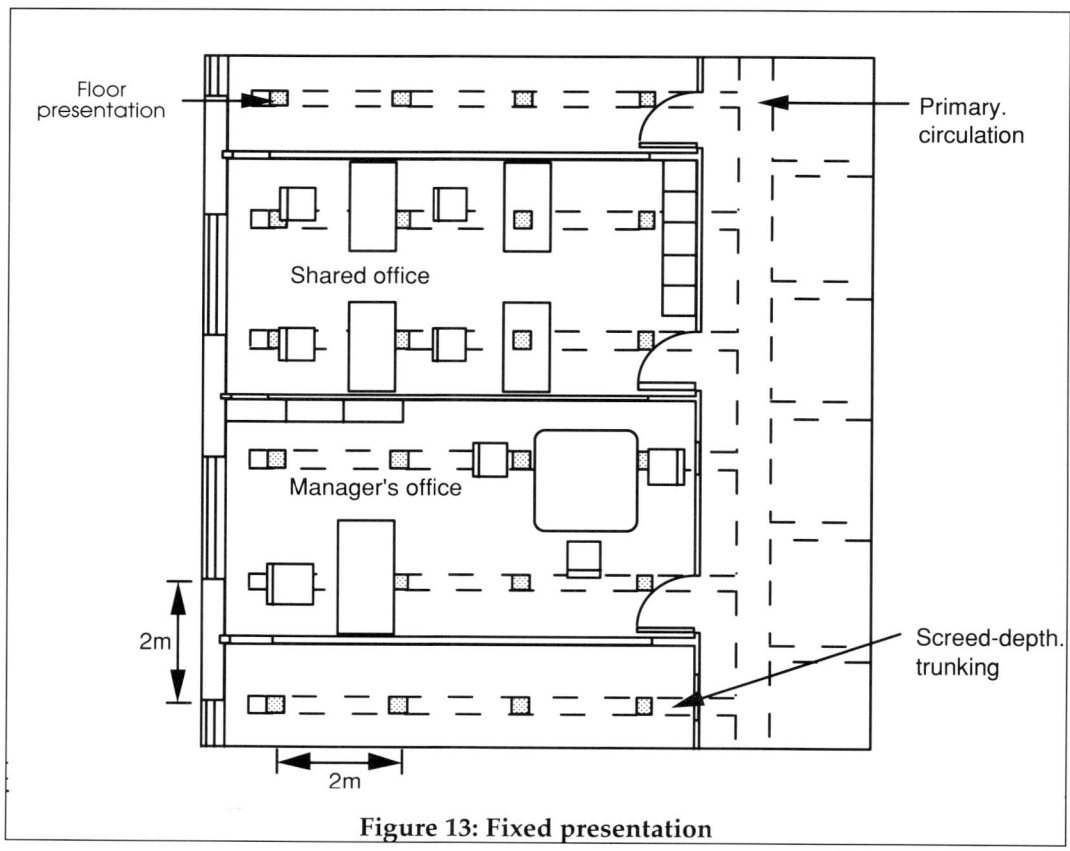

Figure 13: Fixed presentation

Section 6
Quantification

Guidance on the selection of cable media can be found in Section 8, Physical cabling options and design.

6.5 Presentation quantification

Presentation quantification is determining the number of presentations required. Once the number of connections and the types of cable have been determined, it is necessary to specify how they are presented to the user. The infrastructure specifier should look for guidance in the organization's IS strategy documents. If these do not include recommendations, the specifier must consider the options for presentations which are classified into moveable and fixed presentations. As the terms imply, a moveable presentation can be positioned where the user requires it, within limits, whereas a fixed presentation cannot be repositioned. The presentation options can also be limited by the physical constraints of the building.

Fixed presentations

If fixed presentations are to be used, each potential user position must be close to a presentation in order to avoid dangerous and unsightly trailing wires. To avoid constraining the accommodation layout, the ideal presentation density in an open plan or cellular office is one per four square metres, typically effected by installation on a 2.0m grid. Figure 13 illustrates an example of such a system, served by screed trunking and floor boxes.

Moveable presentations

Figure 14, overleaf, illustrates a configuration with moveable floor boxes on a 1.8m grid (chosen to be compatible with the 0.6m tiles of the raised floor). A floor box can be located at any tile position within a 1.8m by 1.8m area, so that it can be positioned under the user workstations. Communications cabling to the floor boxes is shown from an underfloor distribution box serving four presentations, but could also be directly from a telecommunications closet.

The inherent flexibility of moveable presentations often permits a lower installation density than is required for fixed presentations. This is one reason that moveable floor boxes are recommended, in preference to a fixed distribution, when installation is physically possible.

One moveable presentation per six or nine square metres of NLA is often adequate, provided that at least two voice and two data connections are provided at each presentation to maintain the number of connections needed for saturation cabling.

The IT Infrastructure Library
Specification and Management of a Cable Infrastructure

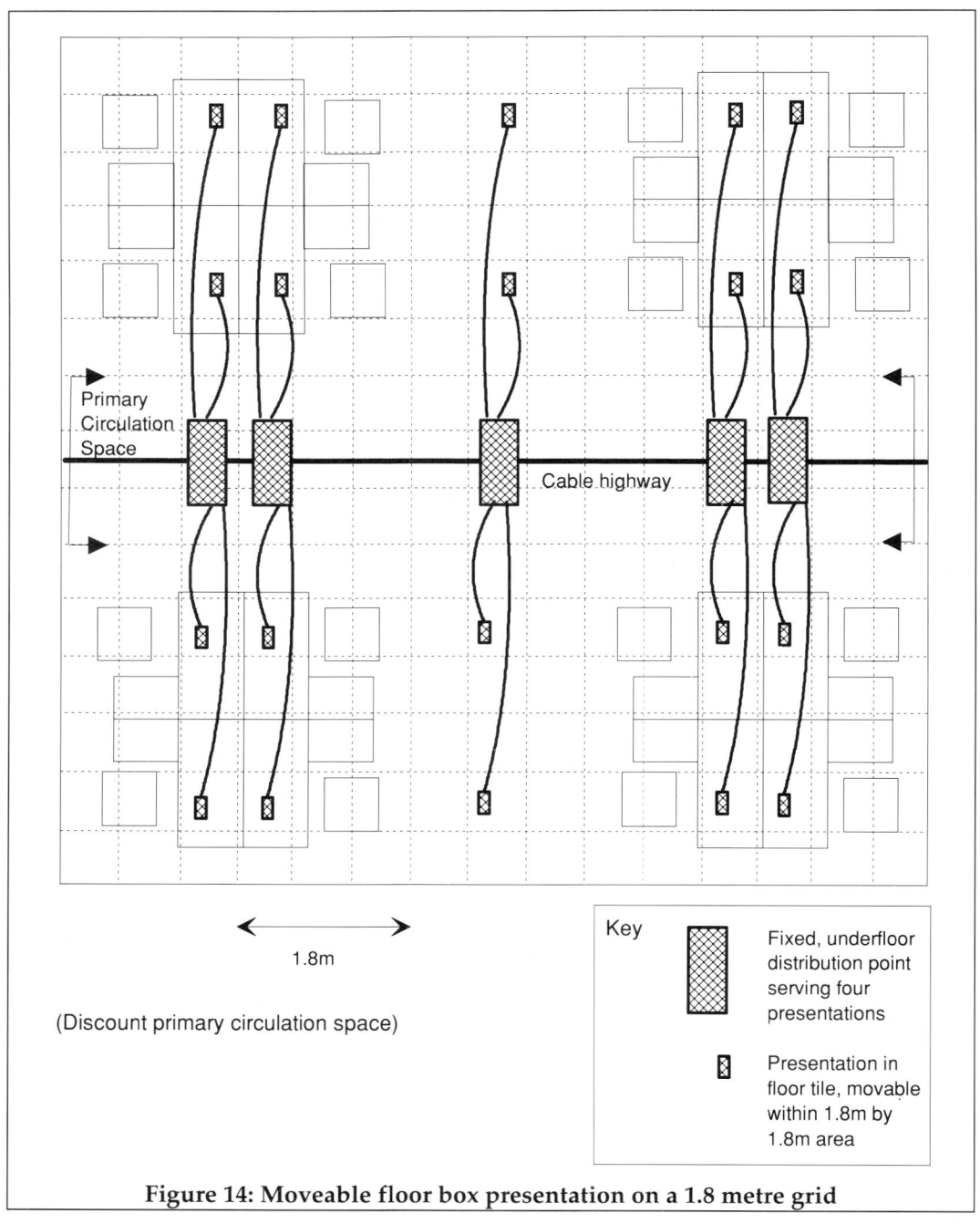

Figure 14: Moveable floor box presentation on a 1.8 metre grid

Further information on horizontal cable distribution is given in section 9.4.

Section 7
Cable topologies

7. Cable topologies

7.1 Topologies should be strategic

The corporate or departmental cable infrastructure strategy should define the topology requirements for local area network (LAN) applications in terms of the physical topology (the way the infrastructure is installed), and the logical topology (the way the infrastructure is configured).

The specifier of a cable infrastructure should be familiar with the strategic LAN and cable topologies, and the ways in which they can be implemented. The strategic LAN and cable topologies ought to be in the organization's strategy statements; implementation is discussed in the remainder of this section.

It is important that the topologies adopted do not act as a constraint on the use of the cabling as a strategic asset and therefore that they conform to an open systems implementation such as GOSIP.

7.2 Physical cable topology

The physical topology of an infrastructure is the layout of the cables and components before configuration to meet user requirements. The physical topology must be able to support international standards and long-term networking solutions, and must have the flexibility required to support the evolution of these communications requirements at different rates within the infrastructure.

Backbone cabling

Backbone cables are used to join a building main cross connect (MCC) to the intermediate cross connects (ICC) and the ICCs to the telecommunications closets. It is recommended that a conventional 'tree and branch' physical topology, referred to as a hierarchical star, should be specified for the backbone cabling. This is illustrated in figure 15, overleaf. The star topology is recommended as it provides maximum flexibility for the implementation of the logical topology, or topologies, through the provision of the cross connects. In a single building, the intermediate cross connects (ICC) will usually be unnecessary, as cables will be continuous between the closets and the main cross connect located in a network room. Only in the largest buildings will it be necessary to use ICCs owing to constraints on cable length.

The IT Infrastructure Library
Specification and Management of a Cable Infrastructure

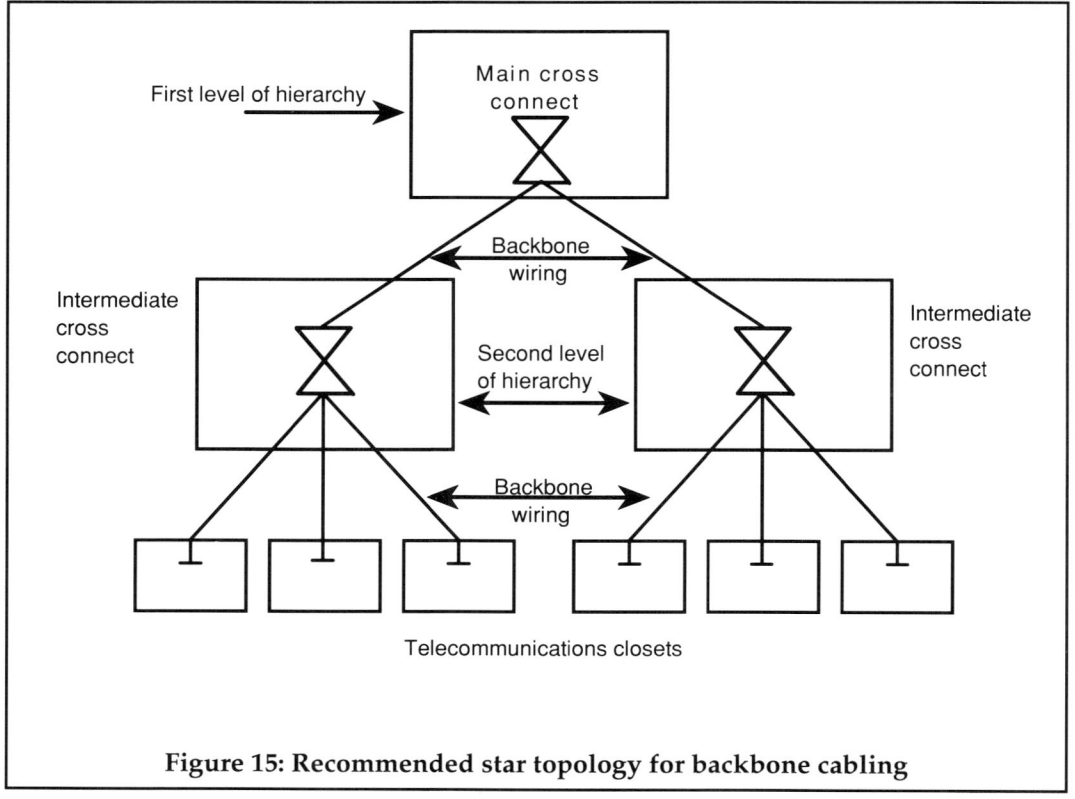

Figure 15: Recommended star topology for backbone cabling

The specifier is recommended to obtain guidance on their use - for example, that given in Annex B, or by including requests for information in the Operational Requirement (OR).

However, when an organization is limiting itself to the tactical implementation of Ethernet only, the installation of 10base5 cables as a bus topology in the backbone is cost-effective and reduces cable lengths. Further guidance on the use of Ethernet may be found in the ISO 8802/3 standards.

The installation of a fibre-optic backbone, supporting Fibre Distributed Data Interface (FDDI), enables a mix of logical topologies to be accommodated easily on the backbone cabling.

Guidance on the choice of cable media for the backbone will be found in Section 8, Physical cable options and design.

Section 7
Cable topologies

Local cabling

Local cabling covers a convenient and manageable section of the building. A star wired topology is recommended, using saturation wiring from communications closets to the presentations. This approach is expanded in Section 6. A star topology is advocated in the EIA/TIA Commercial Building Wiring Standard SP-1907.

In order to conform to the EIA/TIA and Annex B guidelines, each local cable must not exceed a length of 90 metres from closet to presentation, or 100 metres end to end. The implications of this constraint for the accommodation of IT in the building are examined in Section 9, Accommodation requirements.

A star topology is preferred for local cabling as it provides optimum versatility. For example:

* a building can be cabled without the logical topologies being known
* a mix of logical topologies can readily be accommodated
* changes to the logical topology are easy to configure.

Guidance on the choice of cable media for the local distribution will be found in Section 8, Physical cable options and design.

7.3 Logical topology

Alternatives

The physical topology outlined above does not constrain the logical topology to a star configuration. The provision of cross connects and telecommunications closets, as shown in figure 15, also allows the common alternatives of bus, ring, and tree topologies to be configured. If configuring the logical topology is included in the project, the specifier should be aware of the alternatives, how they are formed from the physical topology, and when each is appropriate. The logical topologies are described in the remainder of this section. Factors affecting the choice of logical topology are described in section 7.4, Sensitivities.

Bus

A bus topology as a LAN configuration is included in GOSIP as ISO 8802/3 (Ethernet). The characteristic of a bus topology is that the network devices (computers and peripherals) are attached to a common communication channel (the bus). Data transmission on the bus is by broadcast, and all attached devices receive all the messages on the network (unless it is divided using bridges). The bus communication is managed by an access protocol, such as CSMA/CD.

The IT Infrastructure Library
Specification and Management of a Cable Infrastructure

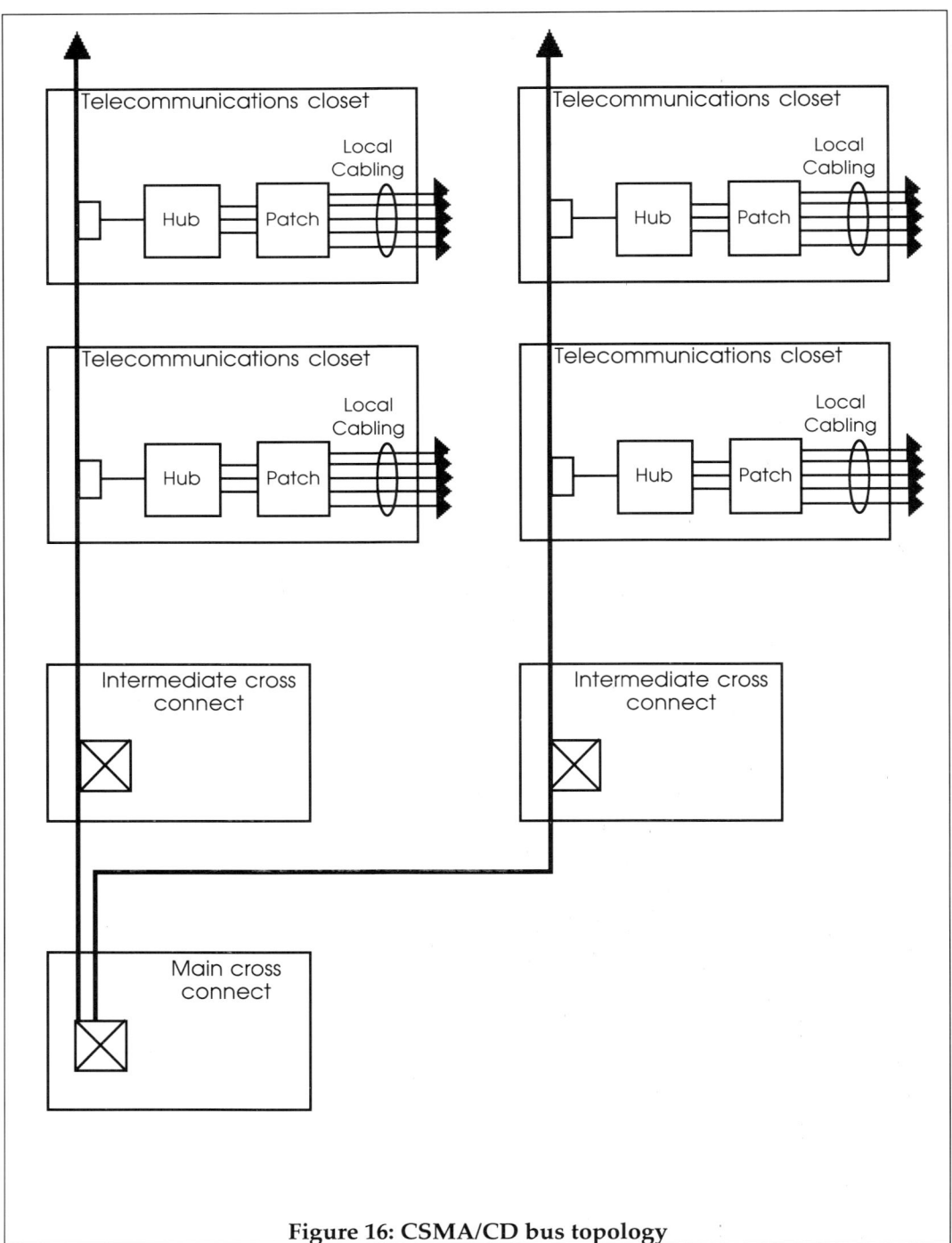

Figure 16: CSMA/CD bus topology

Section 7
Cable topologies

The major strength of a bus topology is its simplicity. Adding or removing devices is easy, and the initial cost of implementing the network is low in comparison to other topologies. The principal weakness of a bus topology is its lack of resilience. A single break in the LAN cable will fragment the network, and may result in the loss of service delivery to many or all of the users.

A physical star backbone configured as a logical bus by patching at cross connects and telecommunications closets is illustrated in figure 17.

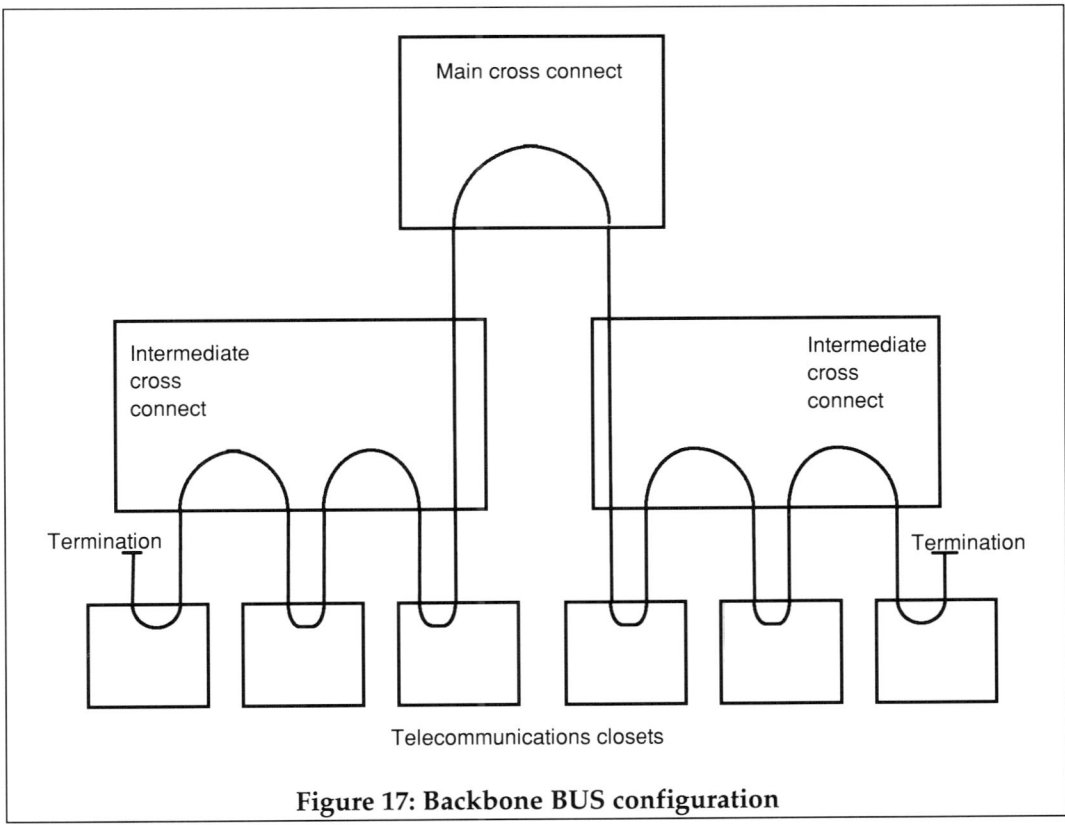

Figure 17: Backbone BUS configuration

Ring

A ring topology is also a LAN standard included within GOSIP, in the form of the ISO 8802/5 Token Passing Ring. A ring network is a collection of user and system devices that are interconnected by cabling configured as a loop.

This topology is more complex than the bus topology outlined above, and its implementation will usually require more cable. A ring is therefore usually a more expensive topology than a bus. However, the resilience of a ring is better than that of a bus, as the ring will automatically reconfigure to isolate a cable break without disrupting service delivery to the users.

The same ability to reconfigure for resilience is also present in a FDDI network. FDDI is a high-speed ring (100 Mbps) using fibre-optic cables, and has been included within GOSIP as an interim subprofile.

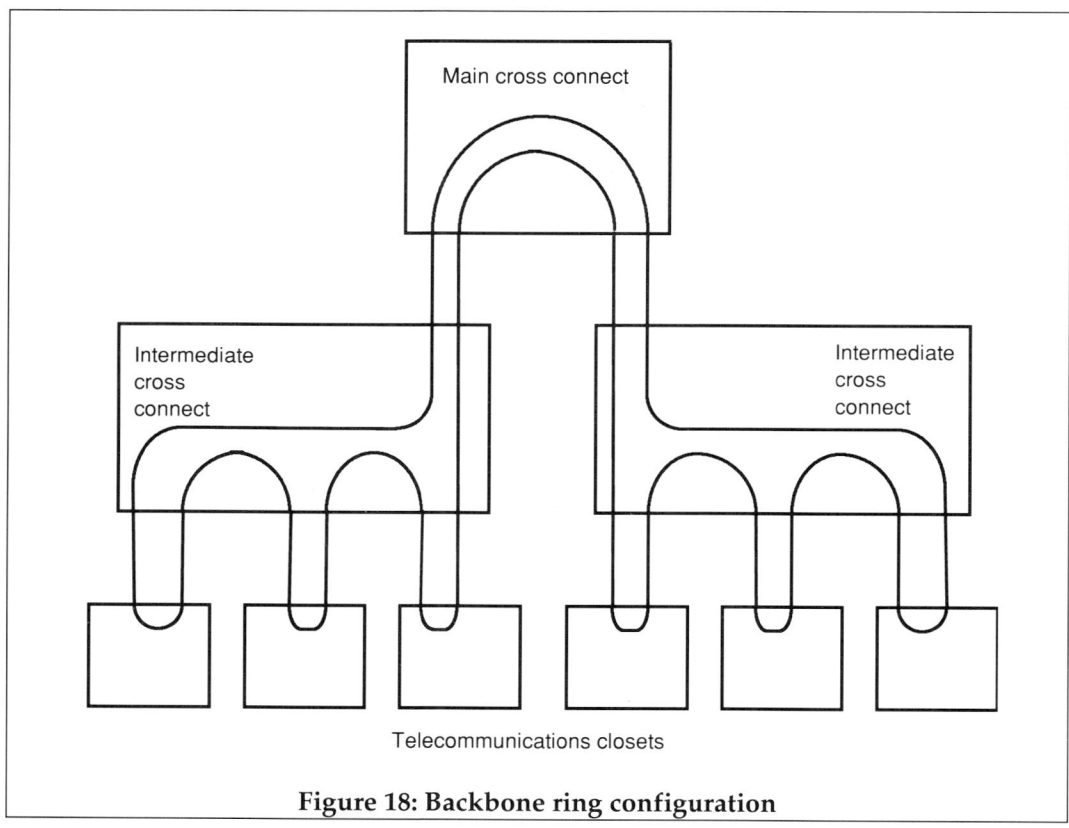

Figure 18: Backbone ring configuration

Figure 18 illustrates a backbone configured to support a logical ring.

Section 7
Cable topologies

Tree

A logical tree topology is readily supported on a star wired physical topology. Examples of its use are for telephone block wiring, and for data connections to a central network room. Resilience is the main benefit of a tree topology since, unlike a bus or a ring, none of the cables beyond the network room carries the full LAN traffic. A cable failure will disable service only to a single user or group of users. Also, unlike a ring, a tree topology is able to maintain a limited service to users in the event of multiple failures since the resilience is not used up by the first failure.

A further benefit of the use of a tree topology is that a high-speed LAN - a ring or bus carrying the full LAN traffic - can be confined to an equipment room. This is a more convenient location for network management and enhances the security of equipment and data.

Both Ethernet and Token Ring LANs can be implemented as physical tree topologies to obtain these benefits, rather than as a bus or a ring respectively.

The configuration of the backbone to support a logical tree is illustrated in figure 19, overleaf.

Specification and choice

The choice of the logical topology will be determined by the requirements for resilience and the constraints imposed by the organization and the building. These factors are known as sensitivities and are dealt with below.

7.4 Sensitivities

The organization's data communications and cable strategies should specify strategic LAN standards that the infrastructure must support, influencing the logical topology adopted. However, the final decision will be determined by a set of requirements and constraints. These are referred to as sensitivities and will include:

* preserving any existing investment
* resilience requirements
* cost
* physical constraints imposed by the building.

Existing investment

An objective of strategic cabling is to provide a cable infrastructure able to support any strategic IT application required during the lifespan of the installation. However, if a major investment has already been made in LAN technology, it may be most practical to continue with the same technology influencing the choice of both the initial physical topology and the logical configuration.

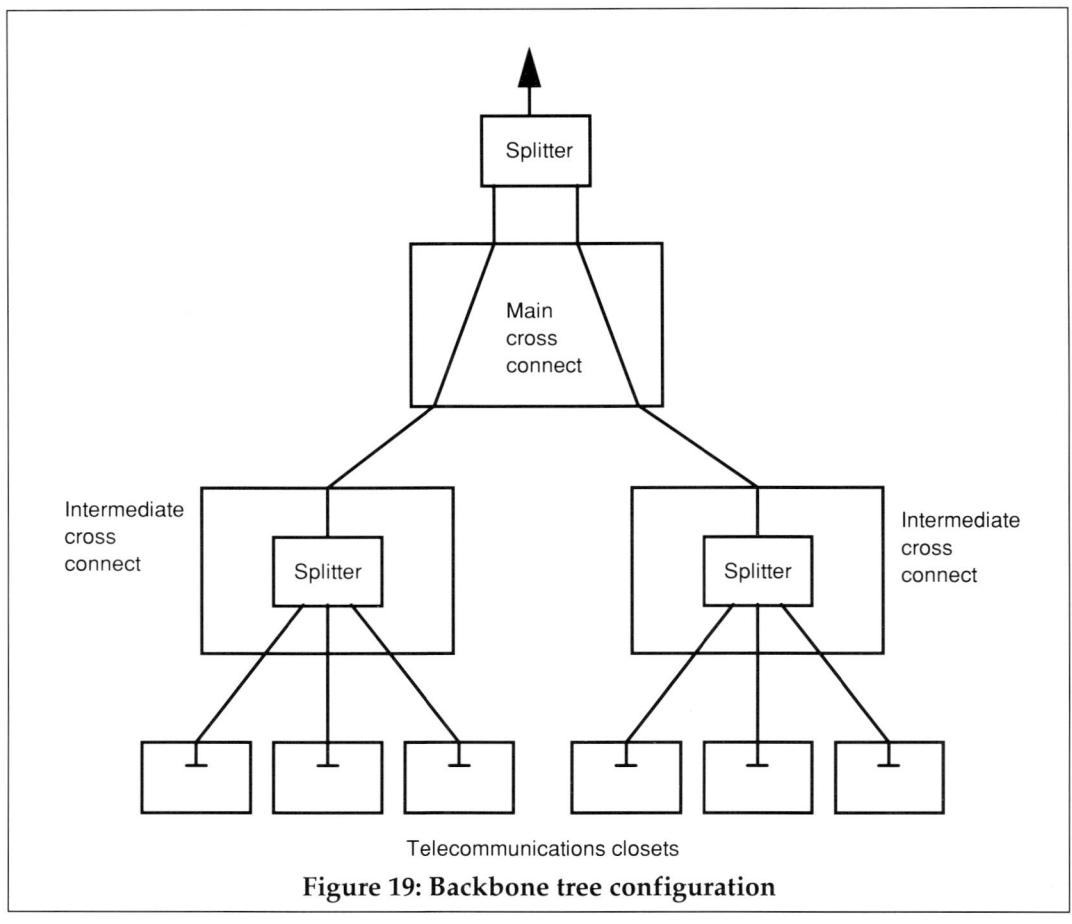

Figure 19: Backbone tree configuration

For example, a bus-based physical topology may be more appropriate than a star to an existing user of Ethernet; and an organization using Token Ring products strategically, and with relatively low resilience requirements, could decide to configure the physical topology as a ring, rather than as a star.

Although the infrastructure can be configured to support existing LANs as outlined above, this should be permitted only for the organization's strategic networks. The infrastructure should not be modified to support non-strategic networks since its ability to support the strategic standards referenced in GOSIP (such as Ethernet and Token Ring) may then be compromised.

Installation of a strategic cable infrastructure is the ideal opportunity to migrate to a totally strategic LAN

Section 7
Cable topologies

installation, and non-strategic networks to be discontinued. Where this is not possible within the time available before a move, then tactical cabling may be installed as an interim measure to support relevant applications - but should be removed at the earliest opportunity.

Resilience

Resilience requirements must be considered when specifying the cable topology. Maximum resilience can be obtained from a star wired configuration, since a failure in a single cable may affect only a single end user. A simple ring configuration offers no intrinsic resilience, as a cable break will interrupt the ring. However, the rings used for Token Ring and FDDI are dual rings and offer some resilience because the ring will wrap around to by-pass a fault, as shown in figure 20. A second break in the ring will cause the LAN to form two small LANS - the resilience being used up on the first failure. A bus configuration has no intrinsic resilience, with a break in the bus immediately fragmenting the network.

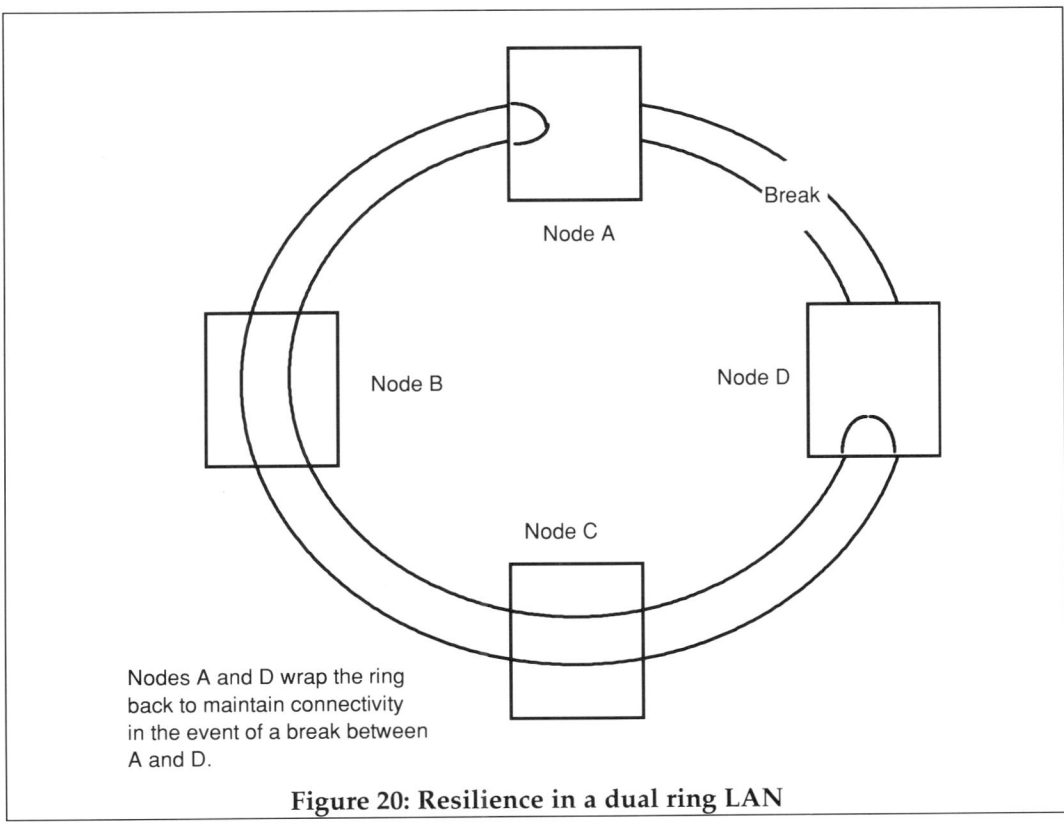

Nodes A and D wrap the ring back to maintain connectivity in the event of a break between A and D.

Figure 20: Resilience in a dual ring LAN

Resilience can be designed into an infrastructure - for example, by the use of the redundant elements discussed in Section 5. However, this will normally result in additional costs, offsetting the cost benefits of a ring or bus over a star topology.

Cost

The cost of the communications cables in an IT infrastructure is usually only a relatively small proportion of the total cost of the IT infrastructure. Cost differences between physical topologies are relatively small, and cost is therefore unlikely to be a significant factor in the choice of topology. Although cabling costs can be reduced marginally by implementing an Ethernet LAN as a physical bus, such implementation would be to the detriment of resilience and strategic LAN implementation.

Building constraints

Although the constraints of a specific building would not normally be considered in the formulation of an organization's overall strategy statements, they must be considered in the specification of a cable infrastructure implementation. The problems associated with both old and new buildings are examined in Section 9, Accommodation requirements. Typical constraints on the topology are:

* inadequate space for the central network rooms required for a tree topology

* lack of space for the telecommunication closets required to provide flexibility in the physical topology

* insufficient riser capacity for a star wired backbone topology

* lack of multiple risers for resilience.

7.5 Sources of further information

Further information and guidance on the subject of this section - for example, in the design of the physical topology - is available in Annex B and from the following references:

* EIA/TIA - SP 1907 Commercial Building Wiring Standard

* BS 89/65578 Standard for LAN Characteristics (Draft)

 (IEC 847 and ISO 7489 are equivalent).

Section 8
Physical cabling options and design

8. Physical cabling options and design

8.1 Cable media options

In the past, owing to the proprietary requirements imposed by suppliers, many different cable media (types) have been used for voice and data cabling. As a result, an organization may have been forced to install many different media to support a multivendor environment. Strategic cabling overcomes this problem by acting as a common carrier between vendors products; the vendors, wishing to retain competitive edge, enable their equipment to operate over the strategic cabling media.

For a strategic approach, an organization must have a standards-based networking strategy and adopt appropriate standards for cabling. As yet, few *de jure* standards exist for cabling, although various standards are emerging.

The EIA/TIA cabling standard and the guidance given in Annex B includes more than one cable medium, and the specifier must choose from the following types which are dealt with later in this section:

* fibre-optic
* coaxial
* shielded twisted pair (STP)
* unshielded twisted pair (UTP)
* ribbon cable (not included in Annex B).

Each cable medium is discussed in detail later in this section, to enable the specifier to select the most suitable media for each implementation. The aspects considered include standards, convenience, performance, costs and security. Security is often a consideration when selecting cables, since they may carry sensitive or classified information.

Annex B6.6, advocates a number of cabling options in support of GOSIP LAN subprofiles, based on a combination of different backbone and local cabling specifications. The configurations are defined in figure 21.

As well as selecting the cable media, the specifier must consider a number of other design options - for example, the types of connector to be used, and the number of circuits to be provided for voice and data in the local and backbone distributions.

Medium	Services Supported	Backbone	Local
UTP	CSMA/CD 10baseT Token Ring Voice	- - S	S F S
STP	Token Ring	I	I
Coaxial	CSMA/CD 10base5 CSMA/CD 10base2	I -	- I
Optical Fibre	CSMA/CD FOIRL FDDI CSMA/CD 10baseF Token Ring	I S - F	- F F F

S = Strategic, where the infrastructure should be regarded as a major investment which will meet long-term data and voice communication requirements over a 15 year timescale;

I = Interim, where there are certain immediate tactical benefits because proven and well established products are readily available, but long term migration problems may be encountered;

F = Future, where the options may be applicable for future strategy, but stable base standards do not yet exist and no GOSIP specifications have yet been developed;

- = Undefined, where the options are considered inadequate for a major long-term investment.

Figure 21: Implementation Configurations

8.2 Voice wiring design

8.2.1 Topology

Star wiring

A star wired distribution should be specified for voice cabling, originating from a distribution frame connected to the PABX test jack frame (TJF), and terminating at the presentations to the users. The typical components of voice cabling are illustrated in figure 22. The use of frames allows any extension line from the PABX to be connected to any presentation, providing flexibility and resilience.

Section 8
Physical cabling options and design

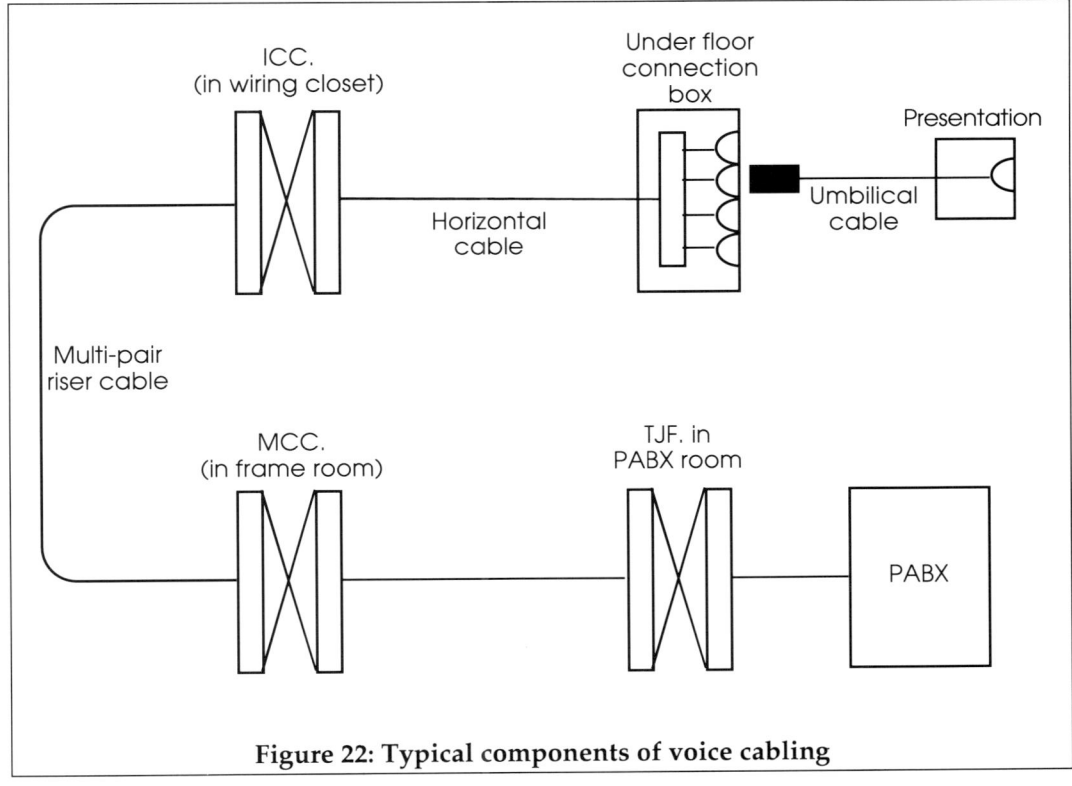

Figure 22: Typical components of voice cabling

Sizing
The specification of a cable infrastructure must include the sizing of the backbone cabling, relative to the local distribution. Saturation wiring often results in the number of connections exceeding the capacity of the PABX. The backbone cables do not therefore need to be sized as the sum of the local cables. As a guide, for most offices, a suitable ratio is 75 per cent. A larger ratio will be required if the local cabling has not been installed on a fully saturated basis.

Number of local pairs
The emerging EIA/TIA standard specifies four-pair cable for the local distribution. Although only three pairs are required for compliance with BS 6701 parts I and II, the provision of the fourth pair is recommended to provide for possible Integrated Services Digital Network (ISDN) cabling standards and some proprietary feature phones, and to permit the same cable type to be used for voice as that for UTP data cabling.

Number of backbone pairs — The backbone cabling for voice should also be specified as four pairs per circuit. This is two pairs more than the minimum required for compliance with BS 6701, in order to provide versatility and to support emerging ISDN requirements.

8.2.2 Media

Local — The local cable specified should be four-pair 100 ohm UTP, compliant with all of the mandatory electrical and mechanical characteristics required by the GOSIP 10baseT LAN sub-profile.

Backbone — The specification for the backbone cable should be as for the local voice wiring, with the exception that larger multicore cables are acceptable to reduce the number of cables to be installed.

8.2.3 Connections

Presentation — The connection offered to the user at the presentation must be specified as a Line Jack Unit (LJU) that meets all of the mandatory electrical and mechanical characteristics required by BS 6312. This is a six-wire connector, and it should be specified that the fourth pair in each cable is left unterminated but available for future use. The use of the RJ45, as used for data UTP, has not been approved for the user connection on voice cabling by Oftel at the time of writing.

Frames — There are three alternative presentations at the frames. These are to use an LJU plug and socket, the data ISO 8877 (RJ45) plug and socket, or an insulation displacement connector (IDC or 'punch down'). The IDC should normally be specified as it is considerably less expensive, more compact, and more reliable than a plug and socket. A demountable connector should be specified only if exceptional flexibility is required.

8.3 Data wiring design

8.3.1 Topology

Guidance on specification of the alternative topologies is provided in Section 7.

8.3.2 Media

There is a wider range of alternatives for data cabling than for voice, with all those listed in 8.1 above being possible alternatives.

Section 8
Physical cabling options and design

To assist the specifier, each alternative is discussed further in Sections 8.4 to 8.8 respectively.

8.4 Fibre-optics

Introduction

The structure of a simple fibre-optic wave-guide is shown in figure 23. Light is transmitted along the core, trapped by total internal reflection at the core/cladding interface and by refraction.

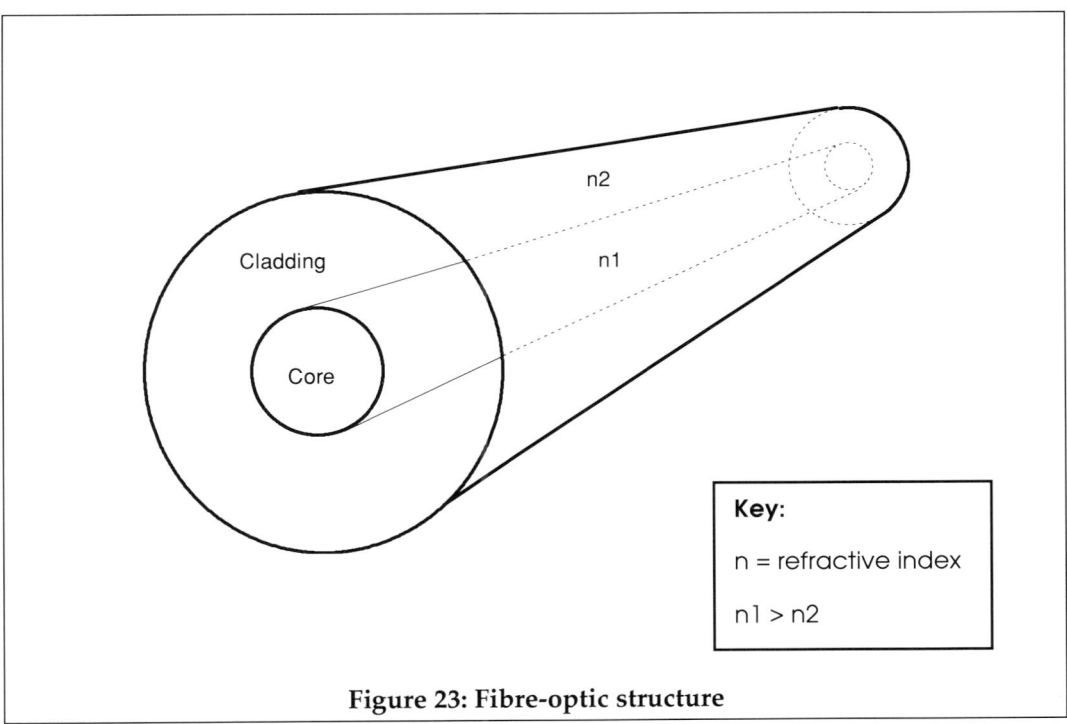

Figure 23: Fibre-optic structure

Recommended fibre

A fibre type is specified by the core and cladding diameters, usually in microns, by its attenuation and bandwidth performance, and by a large number of mechanical properties. A 62.5/125 micron fibre as referenced in Annex B, compliant with EIA/TIA 492 is recommended, with bandwidth and attenuation as shown in figure 24, overleaf.

IEC825

Radiation safety of laser products and systems is covered in IEC825 and BS 7192. These standards are included in the core conditions of CC88 (Part 2-B).

**Figure 24:
Attenuation and bandwidth requirements**

Wavelength (mm)	Maximum attenuation (dB/Km)	Maximum bandwidth (MHz.Km)
850	4.0	160
1300	1.5	500

Standards

Standards for fibre used in strategic cabling are being addressed by EIA/TIA, and these are referenced in Annex B. ANSI and IEEE are also developing standards for data communications based on fibre, for example:

* FDDI (ANSI, Fibre distributed data interface, a 100 Mbps token passing ring)

* FOIRL (IEEE, vendor independent fibre-optic inter repeater link for Ethernet)

* 10baseF (ISO, Ethernet implementation over fibre to the desk).

All these standards specify the use of 62.5/125 micron fibre, and the specifier should refer to the EIA/TIA 492 specification. The use of the main alternative to this fibre, 50/125 micron, although not precluded by these standards, is not considered to be a strategic option.

Although EIA/TIA includes fibre as an option for backbone cabling only, its use is included within Annex B for both local and backbone distribution, in keeping with IEEE work such as 10baseF and FOIRL respectively.

Ease of installation

The installation of fibre is becoming easier as cable and termination technologies evolve. Installation of the cable requires a similar degree of care to that for coaxial cable. However, the fibre termination process requires specialist tools and training.

Concern is often expressed about the bend radii of fibre since fibre ages prematurely when under stress from bending, and develops cracks. These cracks increase the attenuation of the transmitted signal by increasing scatter - reflection of light back along the fibre.

Section 8
Physical cabling options and design

In general, fibre cables have a minimum bend radius of 10 times the cable diameter, or 50 mm, whichever is the greater. This limitation is rarely a problem in a carefully planned and specified implementation, but it is prudent, where physical constraints of the building may apply, to include bend requirements in the OR to ensure that suitable cables are proposed by suppliers. Fibre also suffers from bend loss - a leakage of light from the core into the cladding. Bend loss is a problem that affects mainly long-haul installations, and is not critical for in-building installations when relatively short transmission wavelengths and 62.5/125 micron fibre are used.

Specialized blown fibre techniques are available for cases where there is no immediate need for fibre-optic cables but a future need is envisaged. This technique employs tubing which is installed initially. The fibre is blown into the tubing when required and terminated for use. The cost of procurement, installation and termination of the fibre and terminating technology can therefore be deferred.

Product availability

The market for fibre-optic products has developed extensively over recent years, and products are available to support most of the significant data communication standards, both *de facto* and *de jure*. The strategic data communication options within GOSIP are supported by many manufacturers.

The specifier should be cautious, however, when procuring products for a cable infrastructure that preempt emerging standards such as 10baseF and FDDI station management. Although the products may comply with the ratified standards, this must not be assumed and it would be prudent to include compliance with standards and guaranteed migration towards OSI within the Operational Requirement.

Data rates

The all-silica fibres, such as 62.5/125 micron, have a potential data capacity of hundreds of megahertz over a kilometre - a typical bandwidth length product being 500 MHz.km. One of the main benefits of installing fibre is that the same cable can be used for any foreseeable transmission speed provided that a fibre conforming to the emerging standards has been installed initially.

Line range

The range available from fibre-optic cabling is usually longer than for an equivalent copper cable. For example, run lengths of 2 km are included in the draft of the IEEE 10baseF standards and for Ethernet FOIRL compared to a maximum of 500 m using copper (10base5 coaxial).

The IT Infrastructure Library
Specification and Management of a Cable Infrastructure

Annex B advises a maximum of 2 km of fibre between the main cross connect (MCC) and telecommunications closet (TC) compared to a maximum of 1.2 km for copper (STP). An FDDI network may include a total of 200 km of fibre, with nodes up to 2 km apart.

Resilience and reliability Fibre-optic cable is comparable in price to high-grade copper cables, and cost is unlikely to prevent resilience being included in the installation. Typically, more fibres should be installed than are required, with the spares used to provide backup in case of failure. Fibre-optic interfaces can also be specified with dual power supplies and redundant optical connections to satisfy the resilience requirements of the infrastructure.

Reliability was a problem in early fibre systems as the light emitting diodes (LEDs) and lasers were prone to premature aging. However, reliability is now very good due to developments in device technology and with reductions in the component count in the electronic circuits.

Security Fibre-optic communications offer greater intrinsic security than the use of copper. Fibre-optics are difficult to tap, and the intrusion can be detected by monitoring equipment. Fibre-optics do not generate any electromagnetic emissions that can be detected, and interfaces conforming to TEMPEST requirements are available. When security is important, fibre-optic cable is a natural choice.

Access control The use of laser sources in fibre-optic interfaces is a potential hazard. Normally, the power levels are limited to avoid eye hazard. However, for long-range transmission, it may be necessary to use potentially hazardous transmitters, in which case access control is required to reduce the accident risk. This control must apply to the interfaces and all locations where it may be possible to look at the end of the fibre - for example, at patch panels. The risk is heightened since most lasers operate at a wave-length invisible to the human eye and the hazard is not obvious.

Performance The performance of fibre is superior to other media; it can be used over long distances and cope with higher data transfer rates than copper, and is very versatile in its ability to support different LAN standards.

Integrity A further benefit of fibre is that the optical transmission is immune to electromagnetic interference (EMI). The cables can therefore be routed through areas of high interference without the risk of data corruption.

Section 8
Physical cabling options and design

Connections The connector recommended in Annex B is the duplex connector meeting the mandatory electrical and mechanical characteristics of the GOSIP FDDI LAN interim subprofile. However, the use of other connector types is not precluded, and organizations may find it more appropriate to specify alternatives such as the 'ST' or 'ST II' which are more readily available and at lower cost (particularly for optical patching).

Costs Termination and interface costs are higher for fibre-optics than for copper cables. The termination of spare fibre only when needed, and the procurement of interfaces only in response to user requirements are often cited as ways in which a proportion of the costs can be deferred. Although correct, it would be unwise not to terminate some of the spare fibres, and to have a small number of spare interfaces available, to avoid delays in moves and changes. Cost comparison between the use of blown fibre options and fibre optic cable should be considered.

Summary Strategic backbone cabling must be able to support increasing data traffic as user requirements demand higher bandwidths to meet increasingly sophisticated applications. Fibre-optic cable is the recommended medium to meet this requirement.

At present, the use of fibre-optics in the local distribution is justified in the short term only if its physical properties, such as noise immunity, are important. In the longer term, high bit rate applications, such as 16M bit/s Token Ring, FDDI and electronic document imaging will benefit from the capabilities of fibre, and the use of fibre-optic cables may be justifiable as the basis for such a long-term strategy.

8.5 Coaxial cable

Introduction Coaxial cables are used primarily as a bus, to which terminals and printers are connected, and for video transmission. There is a variety of coax cables available for these applications, and also many proprietary configurations.

Standards Two types of coaxial cable are supported within LAN standards. They both support Ethernet, and are referred to by their implementations, namely 10base5 and 10base2. Both of these cables are included in Annex B as acceptable implementations - 10base5 is included for backbone distribution, and 10base2 for local. However, neither type is a strategic option. The specifier of an infrastructure using these cables tactically should state that cables must be able

The IT Infrastructure Library
Specification and Management of a Cable Infrastructure

to support the GOSIP CSMA/CD LAN implementation. The physical differences between the two types of coax are discussed below.

The use of coax for video, or for terminal connections, is not included in IEEE or equivalent standards, and is a non-strategic solution. The strategic alternatives are fibre, for both applications, or twisted pair for terminal connections.

Coaxial cable is not suitable for Token Ring, and its use within strategic LANs is restricted to Ethernet applications.

Ease of installation

Neither of the Ethernet cables is particularly easy to install, compared, for example, to UTP. 10base5 needs to be handled with care and bend radii carefully controlled. Connection to the cable is easy, but again there are rules which restrict the options. 10base2 is easier to install owing to its smaller size, but access is not straightforward, requiring "T"connections to be inserted into the cable for each connection. 10base2 can be used for star wiring in the local domain, but it is difficult to handle in comparison to UTP. Again, care must be taken to ensure that the installation complies fully with the requirements of the ISO standards, where appropriate.

Product availability

Coaxial cable is well established, and available from most cable installation companies. There is a wide choice of suppliers of the connection devices, including the necessary transceivers.

Data rates

Coaxial LANs will support the nominal 10M bit/s Ethernet data rate. High-grade video coax cables are able to carry bandwidths of about 50 MHz over 100 m.

Line range

The maximum distance supported on a segment of 10base5 compliant with ISO 8802/3 is 500 metres. For 10base2, this is reduced to 185 metres. Larger networks can be created using repeaters (up to a maximum of 4 in series) and bridges. These limits must be considered in the design and specification of a cable infrastructure. Annex B recommends a maximum of 500 m from the MCC to intermediate cross connect (ICC), and also from the ICC to the TC.

Resilience and reliability

The bus topology of an Ethernet installation has no intrinsic resilience. A single fault on the bus will lead to a failure of the entire LAN unless the specification includes partitioning - for example, by the use of intelligent repeaters.

Section 8
Physical cabling options and design

	Reliability is potentially compromised by the requirement for active (powered) transceivers to access the cable. However, Ethernet components are well established, and reliability is unlikely to be a problem.
Security	Coaxial LAN cable is designed to be easy to tap, and security is therefore poor. The screening on both 10base2 and 10base5 reduces the risk of data being intercepted by electronic listening devices. If after risk analysis has been carried out, a specific security requirement is identified, it should be included in the OR and consideration given to use of optical fibre in place of copper cables to enable taps to be detected.
Performance	Coax has been a dependable performer throughout the development of LANs. However, the twin attack of fibre and UTP means that the future use of coax is expected to decline.
Integrity	The cable braiding on coax provides protection from electromagnetic interference (EMI), provided that the braiding is correctly earthed. Earthing is a specialist function and the organization should seek professional advice.
Connections	Connection of coaxial LAN cables should be specified as a BNC connector that meets all of the mandatory electrical and mechanical characteristics required by the GOSIP CSMA/CD LAN sub-profile of ISO 8802/3.
Costs	The use of coaxial cable in an Ethernet environment can be the cheapest in the short term. However, the use of UTP is becoming a less costly way of providing local delivery over a cable infrastructure, with the advantage of greater versatility from a strategic solution.
Summary	For backbone cabling, where a department requires a cost-effective cable infrastructure in the short term only (for example, when there are plans to relocate to a different building) coaxial cable (10base5) would be an adequate, interim solution.
	For local cabling, short-term benefits may also accrue from the use of a coaxial medium (10base2). Products are readily available from a large number of suppliers. However, the medium offers no technical benefits over twisted pair, and should be regarded as interim only.
	The strategic options are a fibre-optic backbone and UTP local cabling.

8.6 Shielded twisted pair

Standards
150 ohm two-pair shielded twisted pair (STP) cable is an interim option in Annex B.

The LAN standard that includes shielded twisted pair, ISO 8802/5 Token Ring, is referenced by GOSIP, and STP is included within the EIA/TIA Building Wiring standard. The use of STP is supported for both local and backbone cabling.

Ease of installation
150 ohm two-pair STP is a bulky cable, which, with its bulky connector, results in large patch panels. As a result, installation is not as simple as for the smaller unshielded twisted pair cables and it is often difficult to accommodate a STP installation within a building. If floor boxes are used for the presentation, they must be specified to accommodate the STP connectors.

If STP is used in the local distribution, particular care should be taken to ensure that access to the communications closets is sufficient to accommodate the massed cables.

Product availability
Products to support Token Ring over STP are widely available. However, product support for other LANs such as Ethernet is more limited.

Data rates
Token ring LANs operate at 4M bit/s and 16M bit/s. Both of these speeds are supported by STP when implemented as specified in the standards.

Line range
The specification should be in accordance with the recommendations in Annex B. These are that the maximum separation between the main cross connect (MCC) and the communication closets should not exceed 1,200 metres, from the MCC to the intermediate cross connect (ICC) 700 metres, and from the ICC to the closet 500 metres.

Resilience and reliability
STP is normally implemented as a ring (configured by patching) or star logical topology. The ring has intrinsic resilience in that it can be severed at one location without loss of service. Multiple breaks will cause the network to split up into a number of smaller LANs. Star wiring provides considerable resilience, since only one connection is made from each cable.

A STP infrastructure should be reliable, because no active devices are required.

Section 8
Physical cabling options and design

Security — The shielding on an STP cable reduces detectable radiations, giving greater security than UTP. However, STP is not as secure as fibre-optic cable, which is much more difficult to tap.

Performance — STP cables are able to deliver a better performance than UTP - for example, in the support of 16M bit/s LANs. However, they do not currently provide a solution for higher-speed LANS, or for long-range transmissions, when fibre will be required.

Integrity — The shielding on STP cables provides protection from electromagnetic interference (EMI), provided that the sheathing is correctly earthed. Earthing is a specialist function, and the organization should seek professional advice.

Connections — The standard connector for data STP is the media interface connector (MIC) that meets all of the mandatory electrical and mechanical characteristics required by the GOSIP Token Ring LAN subprofile.

Costs — A STP implementation is a mid-priced solution, more expensive than UTP owing to the cable and installation cost, but less costly than fibre-optics owing to the lack of active devices and cheaper termination.

Summary — STP is an interim (non-strategic) option for users of Token Ring in both backbone and local cabling. The strategic options are for fibre-optics in the backbone, and UTP for the local distribution.

8.7 Unshielded twisted pair

Standards — Unshielded twisted pair (UTP) is recommended in Annex B for local data cabling only, although included in EIA/TIA for both local and backbone wiring. The cable that should be specified is four-pair 100 ohm UTP, compliant with all of the mandatory electrical and mechanical characteristics required by the GOSIP 10baseT LAN sub-profile specification. This type of cable is commonly referred to as four-pair UTP.

Ease of installation — UTP is easy to install since it is compact, light in weight, robust, and bends easily. The connectors and cross connects are also small - the frames often being wall-mounted to save space.

Product availability	Products are available to support Ethernet and Token ring over UTP although, at the time of writing, Token Ring is often restricted to 4M bit/s. There is a large and growing number of companies able to provide UTP solutions, although the specifier should insist on solutions compliant with standards, such as 10baseT, to avoid being trapped by proprietary products.
Data rates	For Ethernet, UTP will support 10M bit/s data rates - that is, the full network speed. For Token Ring, UTP should be specified at present for 4M bit/s only. Although 16M bit/s data can be carried, the 90m range required for compliance with the EIA/TIA guidelines is not available at the time of writing.
Line range	For local distribution, UTP will support Ethernet and 4M bit/s Token Ring over a maximum 100m cable length (90 metres maximum from closet to presentation).
Resilience and reliability	Star wired UTP in the local distribution is highly resilient, since a cable break will cause a service failure only for the single connection that it serves.
	UTP cabling is resilient, as no active components are required.
Security	UTP offers little intrinsic security since it is easy to tap and also emits radiation as data is transmitted. The specifier of an infrastructure requiring data privacy must specify physical security requirements such as earthed metallic trunking, or select a more secure medium such as fibre-optic cable.
Performance	UTP offers great flexibility in its ability to support both of the strategic LAN standards - Ethernet and Token Ring - and is generally expected to become the dominant medium over the next five years.
Integrity	The disadvantage of UTP is that the absence of shielding means that the cables are more susceptible to electrical interference than STP or coaxial cables, and care should be taken to avoid problems of noise and cross-talk.
Connections	The standard connector for data UTP is the ISO 8877 (RJ 45) plug and socket. This is similar to a voice LJU, but accommodates four pairs of wires. This connector is appropriate for both the presentation and for patching, and should be specified to be compliant with all of the mandatory electrical and mechanical characteristics of the GOSIP 10baseT LAN sub-profile specification.

Section 8
Physical cabling options and design

	Costs	UTP is the least expensive of the strategic media for star wired installation in the local distribution, and offers a highly cost effective solution provided that the data rate limitations do not preclude its use.
	Summary	UTP is not recommended for LAN traffic in the backbone environment, owing to distance limitations and susceptibility to electrical interference.

Local cabling, however, should be unobtrusive, easily managed and flexible in terms of LAN traffic that can be supported. UTP is the cable that best meets these requirements, and is the strategic option for organizations that wish to maintain a flexible approach.

8.8 Ribbon cable

Standards — Ribbon, or flat, cables are not referenced in Annex B, but are not precluded in EIA/TIA as a category of four-pair UTP.

Ease of installation — Ribbon cables are usually straightforward to install in straight lines, but are not easy to route around bends or corners. Power/data cross-overs should generally be avoided.

Product availability — Ribbon cables are available for voice, data and power.

Data rates and range — Data rate and range are often severely limited over ribbon cables because of the priority given to physical design over electrical performance.

Resilience and reliability — Ribbon cables should be used only in the local distribution, which is star wired and therefore resilient since a cable break causes service failure only for the single connection that it serves. However, the way in which they are used, typically under the floor covering, often results in poor reliability. For example, accidental placing of furniture on the cables, or running over them with chair castors, often causes premature failure.

Security — Like unshielded twisted pair, ribbon cables are inherently insecure.

Performance — The performance of ribbon cables is not generally as good as conventional cables, but they can be useful for tactical cabling.

Integrity — Similar to UTP, this cable type is more susceptible to electromagnetic interference than STP and coax.

Costs — Ribbon cables are inexpensive, but do not represent a strategic solution.

The IT Infrastructure Library
Specification and Management of a Cable Infrastructure

Summary   Ribbon cables are not a strategic option, but can provide a useful tactical solution to local cabling constraints.

9. Accommodation requirements

9.1 Accommodation must be planned and specified

The implementation of a strategic approach to cabling, with large quantities of cable, patching and ancillary equipment, makes considerable accommodation demands on a building. An essential element of the specification of a strategic cabling system is therefore space, or accommodation, planning.

Key decisions to be taken when planning accommodation are:

* location of entry points for communications services into the building
* the vertical cable distribution
* the horizontal cable distribution
* the location of communications closets
* identification of equipment rooms and work space.

Suggestions to assist in planning these areas are given below, and the constraints of old (presently or previously occupied) and new buildings are then examined.

9.2 Cable entry points

To reduce the risk of a total loss of service being caused by the ubiquitous pick axe, it is desirable to have more than one entry point into a building for cables from the public telephone operators (PTOs). In addition, there may be cables from satellite or microwave dishes located on top of, or close to, the building to be considered.

Owing to their size and armoured construction, external grade cables often have large bend radii, making them difficult to route within a building. Additionally, to reduce the risk of fire spread, it is prudent to terminate gel-filled cables as near to the building entry point as practical. In order to break out from these cables into indoor grade cables, a small closet or cupboard must be provided close to each entry point.

9.3 Vertical cable distribution

Vertical (or primary or backbone) cables are routed through a building in risers.

The issues

The key issues in riser specification are size, number and location. Others are distribution of services between risers, riser security and the flooring within the risers.

Size of riser

Risers sized on the anticipated number of cables required for a given user population have often become inadequate because future requirements could not be estimated accurately. Riser capacity should also permit replacement cables to be installed and operated while the existing cables are in use. The old cables are removed once the new ones are fully commissioned, ensuring a smooth changeover.

As a design guide, for buildings with up to ten floors of office accommodation, the minimum width of tray for every 100 square metres of net lettable area (NLA) is;

* 15mm for combined voice and network services
* 67mm for data
* 300mm for other services, such as television distribution, and leaky feeders for pagers.

For buildings of over 10 floors, this guideline may lead to excessively large risers, as multiplexing may be used to reduce the numbers of cables required. (Multiplexing is not usually cost-effective in buildings with short cable runs.)

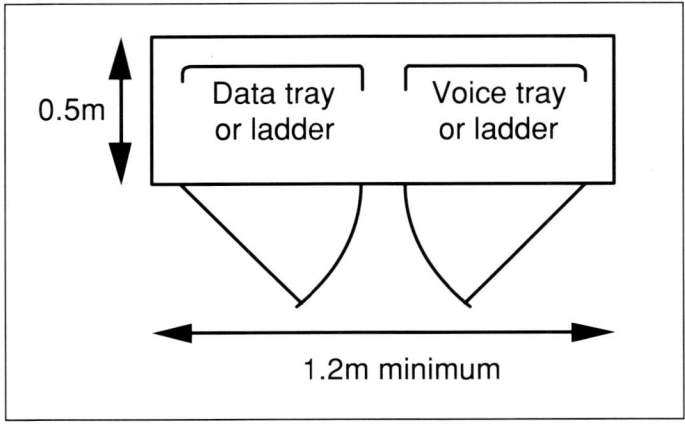

Figure 25: Riser cupboard

Section 9
Accommodation requirements

Owing to this complexity, organizations considering occupying tall buildings should seek specialist advice. The minimum size recommended for a communications riser cupboard is 1.2 m wide by 0.5 m deep, as shown in figure 25, to allow working access. Tapering riser capacity constrains the future location of the networking rooms and should generally be avoided.

The number of risers

Two factors influence the number of communications risers specified for an infrastructure. These are the size of the building (in particular the individual floor areas) and the level of resilience required:

* Annex B and EIA/TIA recommend a maximum 90 metre cable length from telecommunications closet to presentation to conform to LAN operating standards. Since the telecommunications closet will be located in close proximity to the riser, one riser will typically serve a floor area of up to 500 square metres, and a maximum of 1,000 square metres

* resilience requirements may dictate that office areas are served by at least two risers so that a major incident, such as a fire in one riser, will not totally disable service to a group of users.

Location of riser

Riser location will be determined by a number of factors - for example, the constraints imposed by the fabric of the building, the need to be within a 90 m cable length of the users, and the requirements to maintain separation between risers used for dual routeing. Typically, risers are located close to the central service core of a building, where the provision of services to the telecommunications closets is simplified, and the space is less desirable to the users because of the distance away from windows. Access to the risers should also be considered, to avoid disruption to users during network configuration or routine maintenance work.

Service distribution

Distribution of services between risers should be specified by the project team. For resilience, dedication of risers to a single service such as voice, data or power should be avoided whenever possible. It is recommended that communications risers are segregated from those for water, air and power. If this is impossible within the constraints of a project - for example, in an old building - a riser should be used for multiple services and the physical separation of cables and the use of screened trunking should be considered.

The IT Infrastructure Library
Specification and Management of a Cable Infrastructure

Security of riser
Security of risers should be included in the specification. Effective management of a cable infrastructure depends on restricting access to the cabling. Risers should therefore be secure, with controlled keys. Data security is also often a concern, again leading to a requirement for restricted, recorded, access. For a building that may become multi-tenanted, there should be provision for segregated riser space for each occupant.

Construction of risers
Construction of risers may be included in the specification of the cable infrastructure. The riser may be built as a shaft, with infill flooring for safety and fire stopping. Alternatively, lined holes may be drilled through slabs, and the cables threaded through. There are benefits and disadvantages to the IT department of each method. However, the sleeved hole approach is gaining in popularity since the risk of workmen falling is eliminated, cable bundles are kept managed and in line, and the holes are easy to fill with fire-blocking materials.

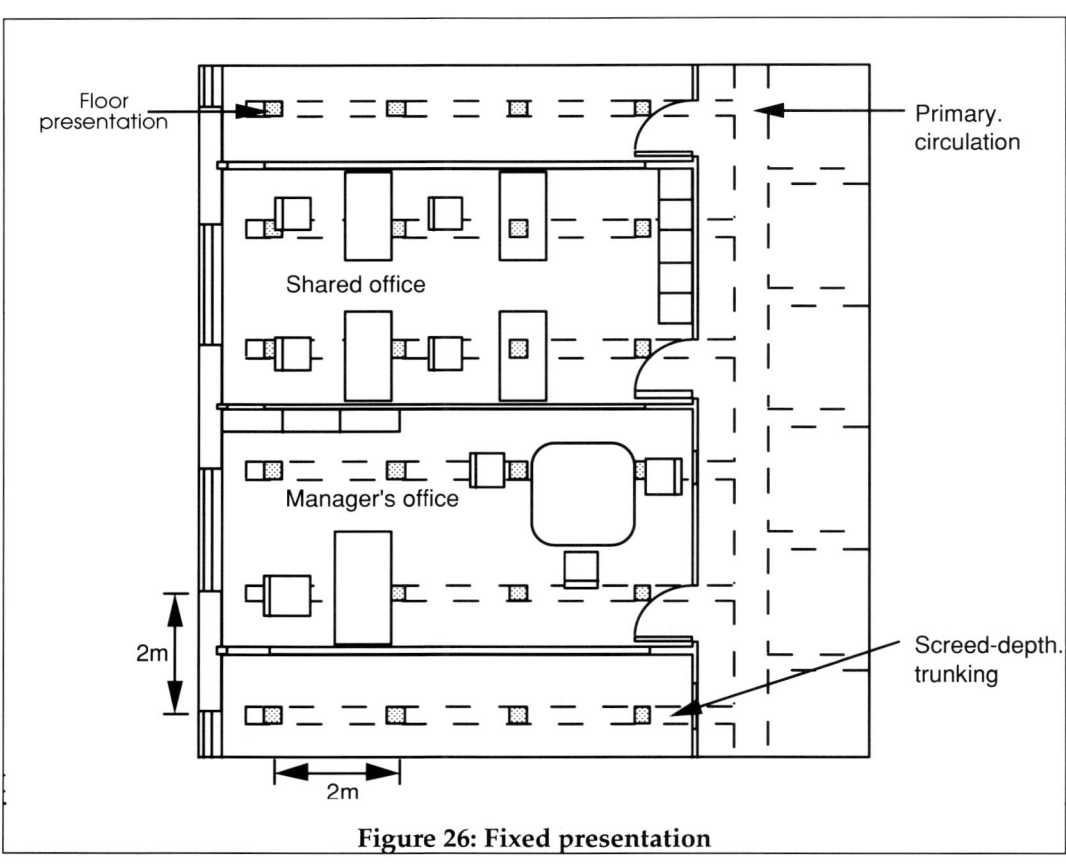

Figure 26: Fixed presentation

Section 9
Accommodation requirements

9.4 Horizontal cable distribution

Alternatives

There are many alternative methods of accommodating the horizontal cabling (also referred to as secondary or local distribution) in a building. The most versatile are those with a moveable, rather than a fixed, presentation to the user.

Fixed presentation systems, such as floor screed trunking, wall trunking, and screens with integral ducts, constrain the location and mobility of the user community. Figure 26 illustrates a fixed presentation distribution. Desk positions are restricted by the locations of the presentations in order to avoid trailing wires to the desks.

Raised floor distribution is the most practicable moveable presentation system; with drop cables from ceiling trays more restrictive, and an aesthetically less acceptable, alternative.

Distribution beneath a raised, or access, floor is recommended since it avoids drop cables from the ceiling, provides easy connectivity to floor distribution boxes at slab and floor tile levels, and allows similar flexibility for power distribution. Figure 27, overleaf, illustrates the use of moveable presentations in a raised floor. The mobility of the presentations enables the desks to be arranged in work groups, without the danger of trailing cables.

Raised floors

In order to allow consistent accommodation planning, it is recommended that raised floors are installed to a common depth throughout the building. The recommended minimum depth is 300 mm. A greater depth may be desirable in areas such as computer suites, where there are high concentrations of cables, under floor cooling, or a need for frequent access. However, where constraints exist and the floor is not used as an air plenum, 150 mm may be adequate for office accommodation where there are no obstructions caused by other building services and where access will be very infrequent.

Communications cables beneath a raised floor may be laid in trays or baskets, or alternatively loose laid along predetermined cable highways. For loose lay, electromagnetic isolation between communications and power cables is provided by distance (600mm is recommended), the cables being positioned in parallel routes. The distribution can often be designed to avoid cross-overs, although they are permissible if bridged and at 90 degrees.

The IT Infrastructure Library
Specification and Management of a Cable Infrastructure

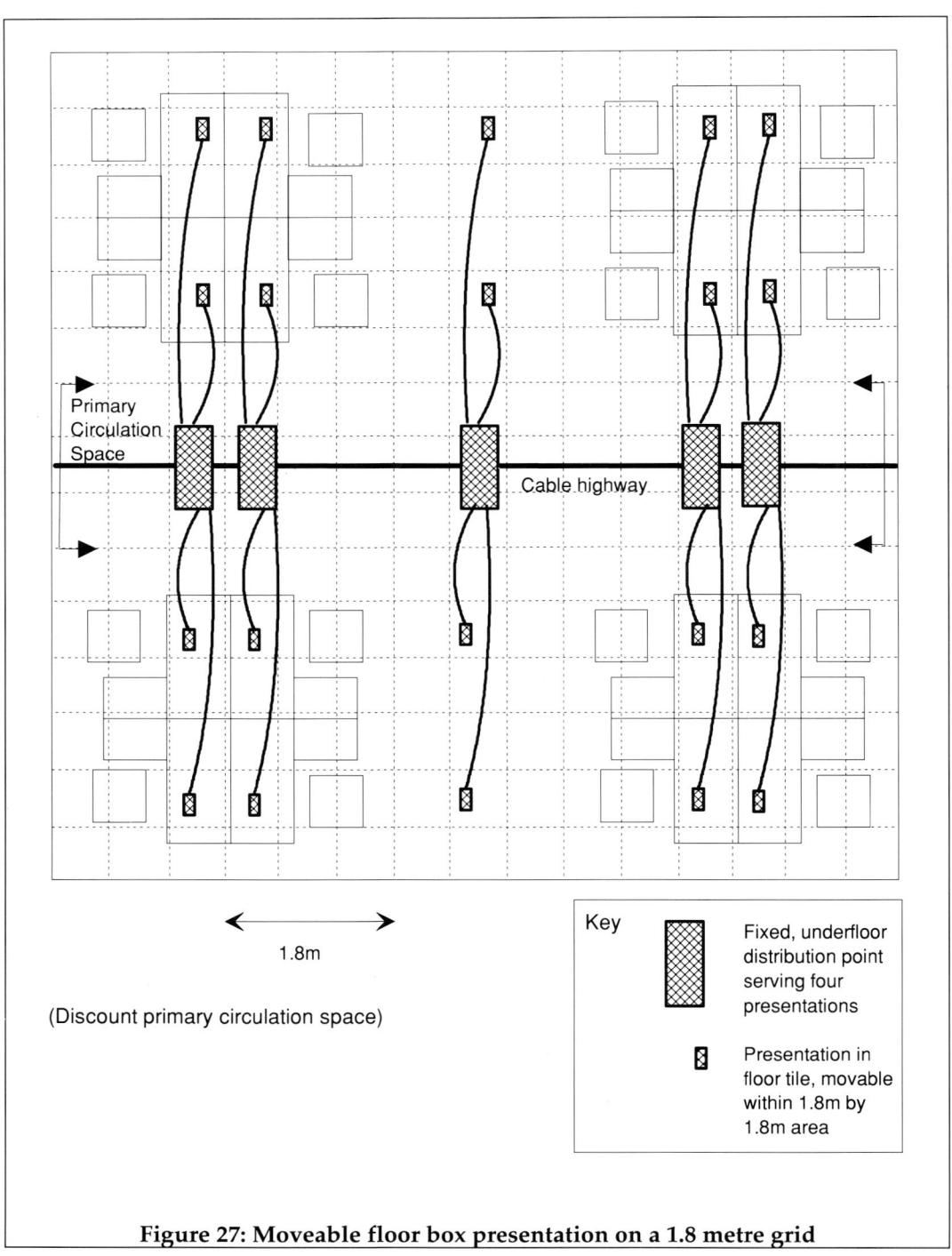

Figure 27: Moveable floor box presentation on a 1.8 metre grid

Section 9
Accommodation requirements

9.5 Communications closets

The requirements

Communications closets adjacent to risers should be designed to accommodate both voice and data communications equipment. Voice requires a distribution frame to connect the horizontal cabling to the vertical cabling. This frame will normally be wall-mounted to economize on space. Data requirements are system dependent, but include patching and network connection devices such as repeaters and media conversion interfaces that are usually installed in stand alone cabinets.

Size

As a guide to accepted practice, a telecommunications closet to serve 500 to 1,000 square metres of office area should be a minimum of 3.0 metres deep by 2.0 metres wide, as shown in figure 28.

Figure 28: Telecommunications closet

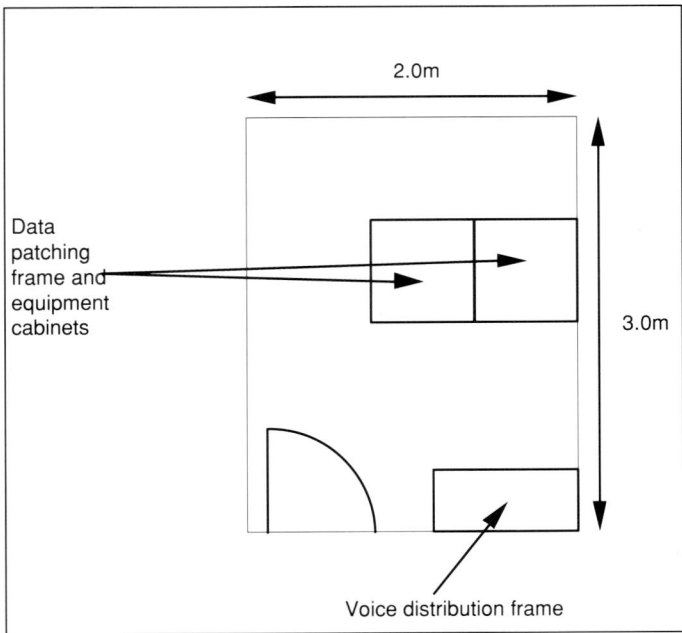

Services

The communication closets should be designed as highly serviced zones with connection to air conditioning and uninterruptible power available if required.

The IT Infrastructure Library
Specification and Management of a Cable Infrastructure

9.6 Equipment rooms and work space

The requirements

The infrastructure specification should include provision, as appropriate, for a PABX room, a voice frame room, and a data network room. The specification of a computer suite may also be included, but is beyond the scope of this module.

PABX room

The PABX room should be designed to accommodate:

* the PABX
* a standby power unit
* a test jack frame
* a desk for an engineer.

CC88 includes minimum environmental conditions, but these may not always be adequate. The final specification will be determined by the PABX selected, and cooling may be required. Lighting should be to a minimum of 300 lux at floor level, and with daylight colour balance to allow wiring colour coding to be clearly distinguished.

Voice frame room

In a strategic cable infrastructure, connection between the lines from a PABX and the extension wiring is made at a building distribution frame (BDF), or main distribution frame (MDF), located in a voice frame room. Accepted practice is to size this room to allow 175 mm of single sided, or 85 mm of double sided, frame per 100 square metres of NLA served. External network connections will be terminated on the frames. Lighting should be to a minimum of 300 lux at floor level. The voice frame room and the PABX room should be physically separated rather than a single room because:

* unlike the PABX, the MDF is a part of the cable infrastructure and may be managed and maintained separately
* telephone cabling may be used for other services in the future
* the PABX may be replaced or relocated during the life of the cabling; a single room restricts the options
* security can be managed more conveniently
* risk of fire damage to frames is reduced
* volume of space needing air conditioning is reduced.

Section 9
Accommodation requirements

Data network room

The data network room is the central distribution point for data within a strategic cable infrastructure. This room will house the main data patching, and, for example, the corresponding pairs of the repeaters and optical modems located in the communications closets. The data network room should be specified to accommodate a similar volume of equipment as the combined communications closets. Owing to the concentration of cabling, the network room should have a raised floor depth of at least 300 mm. Clean power and controlled air conditioning services should be available to service the area as required. Lighting should be to a minimum of 300 lux at floor level.

It is desirable to locate the data network room adjacent to any computer suite in the same building, to simplify the connection of new services to the cable infrastructure.

Location

It is often assumed that frame and network rooms should be located in the lower levels of a building, typically in the basement. There are often benefits to be gained from a higher location:

* maximum vertical cable lengths can be reduced by locating the rooms nearer the middle floor of the building

* security can be improved as it is often easier to restrict access to upper floors

* risk from flood is generally reduced

* it may be possible to use less attractive space, particularly in a building without a basement.

Disadvantages are that:

* risk from fire is increased at higher levels

* building security may be compromised by the access requirements of engineers to the normally more secure floors of a building.

There are also further factors to be taken into account:

* access for bulky or heavy equipment, and floor loading limits, may be restrictive

* M & E provision must be available at the chosen location for power, cooling, ventilation and environmental control.

9.7 New buildings

There are advantages

New buildings offer four major advantages when implementing strategic cabling:

* there may be the opportunity for the IS project team to be involved in the preparation of the architect's brief, ensuring that the building shell will accommodate IT equipment. This opportunity should always be taken. If the organization lacks in-house skills to vet the architect's design, it should consider employing a consultant. The chance to get it right first time is valuable, since the cost and disruption of correcting mistakes can be extremely high:

* building services and fitting-out can be specified and installed to cope with the demands of strategic cabling

* cost of strategic cabling may be absorbed into the overall construction or fitting-out budget

* implementation is not constrained by the requirements of existing occupants.

Fast-track projects

In recent years the high cost of unoccupied space has led to a number of time saving techniques being developed by the building industry, principally in the increased amount of parallel activities to common completion dates. The implementation of these techniques is termed fast-track development. Incorporation of cabling installation into a fast-track development may be attractive in terms of timescales but there are risks, typically:

* the delivery and installation timescales of the cable infrastructure assume greater importance as evaluation criteria

* installation programmes are compressed, for example by out-of-hours working, resulting in higher costs which might not be offset by the benefits of earlier completion

* installation may be required before works services are complete with consequent risk of damage to cables and increasing failure rates of terminations and electronics

* IT installation will be planned in time 'windows' determined by the fitting-out trades; should any delays occur they will have an impact on the IT programme

Section 9
Accommodation requirements

* the time available for acceptance testing and commissioning will be shortened, increasing the need for careful planning and execution of these tasks to reduce the risk of failures when the installation goes live.

The above constraints of fast track development show that it should be invoked only where business needs demand this approach.

Action required

These possible problems from 'fast-track' building development must be considered in the specification process. Management procedures should be required to keep control of work on site, and contingency plans must be prepared to minimize the impact of any delays to the project programme. For example:

* the building works contractor should be responsible for the IT cabling contract, to avoid conflicts of interest when scheduling work on site

* early hand-over of equipment rooms should be planned, since, for example, the installation of a PABX typically takes two months.

9.8 The constraints of existing old buildings

An opportunity

The majority of cable infrastructures are implemented in old buildings that are occupied or may have been vacated. The implementation may be as a part of a major refurbishment, providing an opportunity to remove some of the constraints imposed by the building, or be purely a cabling upgrade with a more limited scope.

The constraints

Typical constraints that an old building imposes on the implementation of a cable infrastructure are that:

* the building may be partially or fully occupied during the works, complicating installation and management

* the floor-to-ceiling height may be limited, reducing the opportunity for the installation of raised flooring

* risers for vertical distribution may be restrictive, or poorly located, constraining the options for cable media, standards conformance, resilience and the ability to install a replacement cabling system before the existing cabling is removed

The IT Infrastructure Library
Specification and Management of a Cable Infrastructure

* space for communications closets and network rooms may be restricted

* listed status, or structural considerations, may prevent improvements in the IT accommodation

* power distribution and capacity may be inadequate

* identification and selective removal of obsolete cabling may be difficult through a lack of accurate records.

Suitability

Following consideration of the constraints, the project board may conclude that a building is unsuitable for the effective implementation of a cable infrastructure. At this point, the organization must make a conscious decision, based on the strategic factors discussed in Section 3.5, either to install tactical cabling or to seek more suitable accommodation. The latter option implies relocation if the organization already occupies the building under evaluation.

Cable audit

If the strategy is to upgrade or selectively replace an existing infrastructure, then a cable audit should be carried out. The audit will identify what cables exist, who is responsible for them, their useful remaining life, and their suitability for incorporation into a new infrastructure. The magnitude and complexity of undertaking a thorough audit should not be under-estimated, as tracing cables is both difficult and time-consuming.

9.9 Sources of further information

Further information about the topics covered in this section will be found in the following references:

* EIA/TIA SP-1907 Commercial Building Wiring Standard

* Cable Infrastructure Strategy

* Modular Computer Buildings

* Environmental Services Strategy

* IT and Buildings - A Practical Guide for Designers.

Full details of these references are provided in Section 18, Bibliography.

10. Provision of environmental services

10.1 Services and cable infrastructures

The physical requirements for the implementation of a cable infrastructure are not simply that adequate space for cabling and interface equipment is provided. Other services need to be specified and installed:

* the number of power circuits
* appropriate quality of electrical power
* facilities for environmental control and removal of surplus heat
* protection against electromagnetic interference (including radio frequency)
* clean earth
* fire protection
* security systems to restrict and detect access.

The project team should ensure that the office environment will be suitable for the intensive use of IT, by liaising with those responsible for the office design.

Many aspects of a building project are beyond the traditional involvement of the IT team. However, it is vital that the IT requirements are taken into account by the services design team, and co-ordinated with the IT specification. There is little to be gained in investing in communications infrastructure if, for example:

* communications cabling is specified to last for ten years but floors have to be lifted after two to install additional power cables
* there is inadequate ventilation which limits the use of equipment closets
* there is standby power for IT but the emergency office lighting is adequate only for the safe evacuation of staff from the building.

The costs to the organization of getting the services specification right will be the time spent in planning and preparing detailed design briefs for the architect or fitting-out contractor, and the increased costs of the fit-out itself to provide for future requirements. However, the cost, in time, disruption and money, of subsequent upgrade of an operational infrastructure is likely to be far greater than extra costs incurred initially.

To assist project team members in communicating their requirements to the contractor, the remainder of this section provides guidance on each of the areas mentioned above. Because of the importance of these areas, the IT Infrastructure Library contains modules giving detailed guidance on the topics. These are referred to in Section 10.8. The following section highlights the implications for the cable infrastructure.

10.2 Power, heating, ventilation, and air conditioning

The designs of power distribution and heating, ventilation, and air conditioning installations (HVAC), have become increasingly interdependent in building projects. They should be planned together. Increasing use of IT requires more electrical power as the use of workstations grows. This power is dissipated mainly as heat, and must be removed by the HVAC installation.

Small power

The power requirements of office equipment, traditionally known as small power, are becoming a major component of a building's total power consumption as IT equipment proliferates. Calculation of the requirements for sizing supply feeds should be based on the maximum number of occupants in the building, assuming that each will require a terminal and a share of printers, copiers and facsimile machines. For an open-plan office environment, this calculation is likely to indicate an average power requirement of up to 40 watts per square metre, or typically an average of 30 watts per square metre of NLA throughout a building.

The small power will be accessed from a large number of 13-amp sockets, cabled as a part of the infrastructure. (Guidance on the number required is given in Section 6, Quantification). Resilience will also influence the small power cabling, in that several separate circuits will be required in each zone of a building. Guidance is provided in Section 5, Reliability and resilience.

Section 10
Provision of environmental services

The specifier of the power distribution must be aware of, and apply, the IEE regulations on diversity in the specification of the small power for an infrastructure.

Computer power   Use of local computers, and the requirements for active (powered) components of structured cabling create demands for highly serviced zones throughout a building. Each of these may need provision of 3-phase power, and as a guide, the feeds should be sized to support an average load of 300 volt-amp (VA) per square metre. It is considered good practice to allow for as much as ten per cent of the building as being highly serviced when estimating total power requirements, although the initial provision may not need to be to this proportion. Equipment power requirements in designated computer suites are expected to reach 550 to 750 watts per square metre, and power supplies should be sized pro rata.

Clean supplies   Although the UK grid supply is normally sufficiently clean at the building intake for IT equipment, it can quickly become contaminated once in a building. For example, lift motors, vending machines, photocopiers and vacuum cleaners can all generate spikes that could affect or even damage IT equipment. Direct feeds from the main intake should therefore be provided to the highly serviced zones and desk supplies. Separation between clean and dirty loads should be maintained by connecting likely sources of interference to wall outlets on a main circuit separate from the small power distribution.

To avoid dirty loads being inadvertently connected to the wrong circuit, it is recommended that the clean supplies are fitted with a different plug and socket from the standard 13-amp sockets used for the dirty supply.

Secure supplies   Two levels of power supply continuity can be specified. The first is protection by a standby system such as a diesel generator. When it is important that there are no breaks in the supply, or if the quality of the locally generated supply is unacceptable, the second level of protection, an uninterruptible power supply (UPS), will be required.

To enable an organization to function effectively in the event of a mains supply failure, it is essential that the generator capacity is sufficient to support all essential services. These will include lighting, terminals, computer suites, highly serviced zones, and a proportion of the HVAC installations.

In the past, an UPS was not usually specified outside the computer suites. However, the growth in the use of local disc units and of active devices in the cable infrastructure creates a demand for UPS elsewhere in a building. In addition, there may be specific user applications that require UPS, such as security, trading or reservation systems. However, since large UPS installations are expensive, the benefits must be weighed against the costs.

HVAC

The requirement for increased HVAC provision to remove surplus heat from office areas is one effect of the increased use of IT. It follows that the HVAC service is also critical to business operation. An air conditioning failure could prevent the business from working if systems are shut down to prevent heat build-up in computer suites or communications closets. As HVAC underpins the IT infrastructure, the availability of HVAC must be planned and managed, as discussed in Section 5, Reliability and resilience.

Office 'hot spots'

The capacity of the HVAC installation must be sufficient to remove the heat generated by IT equipment, in addition to the normal loads caused, for example, by occupants, lighting and solar gain. The IT heat will be approximately equal to the average power requirements previously indicated in this section, although the HVAC must also be designed to prevent local hot-spots occurring. In an office, the HVAC must be able to remove the heat from local concentrations of IT equipment, typically 166 watts per square metre over an area of 6 square metres.

Increased demand for HVAC may result in larger ducts than previously planned or installed in a building, and this must be considered when the sizes of the services risers and horizontal distribution are specified.

10.3 Electromagnetic interference

Electromagnetic interference (EMI) is a potential cause of major problems in a cable infrastructure and care must be taken to prevent difficulties occurring.

Requirements for clean power supplies for IT, and the desirability of separating power and communications cables in risers are detailed in sections 9.3, 9.4, and 10.2 of this module. Further guidelines for controlling the effects of interference on cabling and IT equipment are:

* live and neutral conductors should be kept close together - for example, in lighting circuits

Section 10
Provision of environmental services

* power cables installed parallel and in close proximity to communications cables should be segregated in earthed metal trunking, or sheathed with earth bonded wire braid armour

* the installation of computing equipment in line of sight to sources of radio frequency interference (RFI) such as radio or radar transmitters should be avoided.

Development of faster computers is likely to result in machines with greater sensitivity to RFI than those used at present. With the increase in building development in the vicinity of air and sea ports, the potential problem of RFI is likely to be of concern to increasing numbers of organizations. The problem is that, even after specialist electromagnetic surveys have been carried out, it may be difficult to obtain assurances from suppliers that interference will not cause failures or corrupted data. A further complication is that future events, such as the building of a new radio transmitter, cannot be predicted - the only protection is the installation of expensive RFI shielding for computer suites or even for the entire building.

The EC Directive EC 89 336 on electromagnetic compatibility will place certain responsibilities on users. Although suppliers will be responsible for susceptibility requirements, users will be responsible for emissions. The Directive places responsibility on the user to ensure that an overall system complies with the requirements. It should not be assumed that, even if all the components of the system are individually compliant, the system will conform.

The specifiers of an infrastructure should be aware of their responsibilities. Further guidance is available from the IT Infrastructure Library module **Management of Electrical Interference**.

10.4 Earthing

Earthing is important for electrical safety, for electromagnetic screening and also in telephony applications for signalling.

Safety

Since the prime consideration must be safety, earthing of IT equipment should be to IEE wiring regulations.

Screened cables

The use of power cables with an earthed screen or in earthed trunking is recommended when they are installed parallel to communications cables.

Some IT manufacturers also recommend the use of screened data cables to prevent interference corrupting data and to reduce RF emissions from the cables. Earthing requirements vary between systems, and they should therefore be installed as directed by the supplier. However, since shielded twisted pair cables are not a recommended strategic implementation (see Section 8, Physical cabling options and design), it is suggested that an organization view their use only as a tactical solution. The infrastructure should be planned to eliminate the sources of interference and not to mitigate the effects.

Clean earth

Suppliers' requests for dedicated noise-free earths for IT equipment in the office environment should be resisted. They undermine the universal nature of the cable infrastructure. Separation of dirty loads from the IT supply, as recommended in the discussion on power distribution in section 10.2, will normally be adequate in these circumstances. In highly serviced zones, connection to the building intake will provide a sufficiently clean earth for most computer equipment.

Earth recall

An earth connection may be required between a telephone instrument and PABX to operate earth recall signalling. For implementation, an earth cable will be required from the PABX to each telecommunications closet, where it will be connected to the cabling from each instrument. It is important that this earth is connected to the safety earth only at a single point, usually at the power intake main distribution.

Lightning

Running lightning conductors down a riser within a building is no longer considered a safe practice. Even if the current does not arc to other cables, the conductor may induce current in communications cables in the riser, resulting in damage to equipment. Any external communications cable that extends beyond the zone protected by lightning conductors, even if buried, should be fitted with a surge protector.

10.5 Fire protection

Protecting the fabric and structure of a building is not usually the responsibility of the IT project team. However, the IT installation is an important consideration in planning fire prevention and protection. Consideration should be given to avoiding the incidence of fire, reducing its spread, and minimizing its damage.

Section 10
Provision of environmental services

Many IT fires begin with underfloor cables slowly overheating. Underfloor smoke detectors, and detectors in the intake and outlet ducts of air handling units, increase the probability of detecting any smouldering before a fire develops and takes hold. To avoid the spread of fire, it is important that risers are blocked between floors, and that fire barriers beneath raised floors are restored after cables have been installed.

In addition to the hazard to personnel, the smoke and corrosive gases given off by burning PVC coated cables can damage computers and other equipment. Consideration should be given to specifying what is known as a low-smoke, low-fume cable sheathing in sensitive areas.

10.6 Security

Controlled access to IT installations is important for three reasons:

* operation and management of the infrastructure must be maintained by a single authority

* the risk of accidental or deliberate damage to, or theft of, equipment must be minimized

* data may be classified or sensitive.

Examples of the security steps that may be taken by an organization which affect cabling are:

* segmentation of the computer room into smaller rooms with restricted access

* locking and restricting access to risers.

Access control to all elements of the IT infrastructure, including the cabling, should be managed from a central point to avoid errors and to create a clear procedure.

For cost effective protection of systems and data, CCTA has produced a risk assessment method known as CRAMM. It is a software-based tool to locate weaknesses in the existing security arrangements and to assess the required security level according to the business operations and the risks that the organization is prepared, or permitted, to take.

Any organization processing, storing or transmitting classified information must approach the relevant security authorities to obtain advice on protecting that information.

10.7 Lighting

Guidelines for lighting in network and telecommunication rooms is provided in Section 9, Accommodation requirements. However, the IT infrastructure team should also have an influence on the lighting design for the office environment. The effective operation of screen-based terminals requires a lower level of illumination to improve screen display contrast than that normally provided in an office. However, the user is also likely to carry out paper-based tasks requiring the higher intensity level on an occasional basis. Further problems are avoiding glare and reflections.

The normal solution to illumination levels is the provision of diffuse background lighting, supplemented by task lighting from individual desk lamps. This allows maximum flexibility in the office layout since desk locations are not determined by fixed task lighting.

The implications for cabling are that:

* lighting power circuits must be installed without causing interference (see 10.3 (EMI), above)

* power must be available at each desk for the task lighting

* data cables must be kept away from sources of interference - for example, from fluorescent tubes.

10.8 Further information

Further information on the topics covered in this section can be obtained from the following IT Infrastructure Library modules:

* Accommodation Specification
* Environmental Services Strategy
* Fire Precautions in IT Installations
* Management of Electrical Interference
* Managing a Quality Working Environment for IT Users
* Office Design and Planning
* Secure Power Supplies.

Section 11
The structure of the Operational Requirement

11. The structure of the Operational Requirement

11.1 Why use an Operational Requirement?

The cable infrastructure Operational Requirement (OR) is a document that states the requirements of the organization and of the proposed cable infrastructure, and includes many of the aspects already discussed in this module, such as quantification, topologies, reliability and management.

The OR follows the development of the cable strategy, drawing on it for the specification of the cable requirements and is the first formal contact with potential suppliers in the procurement process. The OR will normally lead to:

* proposals from suppliers
* shortlisting
* Memorandum of Agreement (MoA)
* Invitation to Tender (ITT)
* tenders from suppliers
* contract.

IS Guide B6 **Procurement** provides guidance on these procurement processes.

Objectives

The objective of the OR is to help obtain the best value for money. Value for money should not be judged solely on the basis of lowest tendered price. The most cost-effective solution may not be the cheapest tender, since cost penalties for failing to meet desirable requirements and the long-term benefits must also be considered. Factors such as design, reliability and maintainability will also affect the total cost over the life of the infrastructure.

Purpose of the OR

The purpose of a cabling OR, as with any other, is to express the organization's business needs so as to draw the best solutions out of the IT industry in the interests of the organization. Suppliers submit proposals of the way in which their products and services can be used to meet the needs specified by the OR. The OR therefore describes the job needing to be done, not the means of achieving it; it is not an ITT.

The OR serves a number of detailed purposes:

* it provides potential suppliers with details of project requirements so that, if they consider it worth their while investing effort in bidding for the business, they can submit proposals of how their products or services would meet those requirements

* it provides the basis for evaluating those proposals and selecting a shortlist of potential suppliers to proceed to detailed discussion

* it acts as the definitive reference during discussions to ensure that all bidders' proposals are dealt with on an equal footing and is also the basis of tender evaluation (see section 12, Evaluation).

There are a few circumstances, notably in the procurement of very small cable infrastructures, where it may be appropriate to proceed straight to the ITT without issuing an OR. IS Guide B6, **Procurement** provides guidance on this topic.

11.2 What makes a good OR?

Since the OR is a statement of the organization's needs, it is vital that the requirements are comprehensive. They must also be complete, consistent, unambiguous and verifiable. The OR then allows potential suppliers to propose solutions that use their particular products to best effect in meeting the stated requirements, rather than a general solution.

The OR must focus on the business needs of the project, rather than on any perceived technical solution. Except for single tender procurements, it should not be biased towards any particular supplier.

11.3 What should an OR look like?

An OR will contain three main sections:

* setting the scene
* stating the requirements
* rules for suppliers.

The typical content of each of these sections, for a cable infrastructure OR, is expanded below.

Section 11
The structure of the Operational Requirement

11.4 Setting the scene

Purpose

The OR should start with a short section, typically between two and three pages, telling potential suppliers what the organization does in business terms, how this requirement fits into its work, and what its future plans are. The organization's LAN and cabling strategies, and how this OR relates to them, should also be described. If the proposed requirement is to replace or upgrade existing cabling, the introduction should describe the current installation and proposed changes.

The three standard sections when setting the scene in a cable infrastructure OR are:

* Introduction
* IT infrastructure standards
* Information and constraints.

11.4.1 Introduction

The introduction gives suppliers an outline of the project so that they can decide whether or not to become further involved, and it should place the requirement in the business context. The introduction should contain the following information:

* the objectives and scope of the project
* the tasks to be undertaken
* the project locations and timetable
* reference to other policies that have an impact on this OR - for example, the IS and cable strategies
* the purpose and structure of the OR document.

11.4.2 IT infrastructure standards

This section must set out the main points of the IS and cable strategies, and describe the IT services that the infrastructure must support. The specifier should include:

* strategic network standards to be supported (for example, Ethernet and Token Ring)
* strategic cable media (for example UTP, fibre optic)
* computer equipment to be connected (where known).

11.4.3 Information and constraints

This section must include any information that will help the suppliers to understand the particular project to which the OR applies, background information and specific constraints. Examples are set out below.

The size of the infrastructure

The supplier will need to know:

* the number of buildings
* distances between buildings, if more than one
* dimensions and numbers of floors
* height between floors (slab-to-slab and floor-to-ceiling)
* areas to be cabled for immediate use
* areas to be provided with cables for deferred use.

Backbone distribution

Information should be provided on:

* routes between buildings
* cable entry points into each building
* riser locations, design, size, services and available capacity
* locations and size of network, PABX and frame rooms and closets, or the space available
* power, environmental services, and cable routes to, within and from the computer rooms and closets.

Local distribution

The suppliers should be made aware of:

* provision and specification of raised floors if not part of this procurement
* availability of wall, floor or ceiling routes
* type of existing presentations, if they are to be retained
* the numbers of existing presentations and distribution or saturation density.

Proposed facilities   The supplier should be told of the availability of facilities such as:

* onsite storage space and security
* office facilities such as desk and telephone
* 240V/110V power.

11.5 Stating the requirement

In this section, the specifier must provide a detailed logical specification of the requirements that will allow the suppliers to produce a design and costing. The content of this section will vary according to the scope of the project, but must set out all of the requirements. A suitable format for this section, following the recommendation of IS Guide B5, **The Operational Requirement**, is:

* infrastructure requirements, including
  - mandatory requirements
  - desirable requirements
* timetable
* further information required from suppliers.

11.5.1 Infrastructure requirements

This section will form the core of the OR, and must contain all the requirements of the cable infrastructure. It should start with an overview of the requirements, before setting them out in detail. The requirements should be separated clearly between mandatory requirements (without which it would not be viable) and desirable requirements (additional benefits). For clarity, mandatory and desirable requirements will usually be separate sections of the OR, with each requirement numbered for ease of reference. The requirements are described in other sections of this module. The specifier must decide which are mandatory and which are desirable for a particular infrastructure; typical examples are set out below.

Mandatory requirements Typical categories of mandatory requirements for a cable infrastructure are:

*	Standards	All standards that must be followed
*	Environmental	IT equipment thermal emissions and noise levels
*	Security	Restricted areas, access controls
*	Resilience	Requirements, not method of provision
*	Service levels	Ability to meet required reliability and serviceability criteria
*	Topology and media	Conformance to organization's strategy
*	Project management method	Minimum requirements of tools and techniques
*	Component and cable marking	Conformance to minimum acceptable procedures
*	Cable management tool	Provision of tool meeting minimum specification acceptable
*	Design	Strategic media; presentation layout and density; quantification
*	Testing	Compliance to specified procedures and resulting documentation (see Section 13, Commissioning and acceptance testing)
*	Programme	Ability to meet required dates within project constraints, such as restricted access or limited working hours.

Section 11
The structure of the Operational Requirement

Desirable requirements

Requirements should be presented as desirable whenever possible, since mandatory requirements can be restrictive or costly. Requirements may overlap classifications - for example, there may be both desirable and mandatory size limits for items of equipment. Typical desirable requirements will be:

*	Specific project management method	For example, use of PRINCE
*	Maintenance	For example, of existing equipment or use of existing maintainers
*	Connectors	Preferred types not covered by mandatory standards
*	Component identification	Full conformance to proposed scheme
*	Standards	Conformance to other, non-mandatory, standards
*	Design	Higher saturation density; more connections per presentation
*	Facilities	Ability to work with proposed facilities only
*	Environment	Suitability of proposed environmental services
*	Specific commissioning and acceptance testing	Tests beyond the minimum requirement
*	Cable management	Use and post-implementation support (if not mandatory).

11.5.2 Timetable

Details of the project timescales should be included, and critical dates highlighted. A list of timetable elements can be found in IS Guide B5, **The Operational Requirement**.

105

11.5.3 Further information required from suppliers

This section allows the specifier to seek additional information - for example, the supplier's policy on intercepting emerging standards (such as FDDI and 10baseF) - and to support the organization's migration policy. Suppliers should be given an opportunity to add comments on other features of their solution not brought out in the requirements sections.

11.6 Rules for suppliers

This section is used to tell the suppliers what is required in response to the OR. For simple cable infrastructures, it may be possible to incorporate all the requirements in the main body of the OR, although most will justify the inclusion of detailed compliance statements as Annexes.

It is much easier to compare and evaluate proposals when they are submitted to a common format, and this requirement should be stated in the OR. It is particularly important that information specifically requested is separated from any additional information the supplier decides to provide. A standard format for proposals submitted in response to an OR is listed below as an example. The specifier of the OR will need to consider carefully whether further information is also required, and include sections as appropriate.

1. Management summary
2. Point-by-point statement of compliance with mandatory requirements
3. Point-by-point statement of compliance with desirable requirements
4. Description of proposed infrastructure
5. Timetables
6. Hardware configuration
7. Proposed software and availability
8. Maturity of proposed system components
9. Software packages (if appropriate)
10. Loading/sizing summary

Section 11
The structure of the Operational Requirement

11 Levels of serviceability/reliability

12 Supporting services

13 Costs

14 Further information.

Each of these sections is expanded below, highlighting the information required from the prospective suppliers.

11.6.1 Management summary

The supplier's approach and plans should be summarized, highlighting important features and the cost of the project. The approach should include a brief description of the cable media and topologies proposed.

11.6.2 Mandatory requirements

The supplier must indicate how each mandatory requirement included in the OR will be met - for example, compliance to standards (IEEE, EIA/TIA) and guidelines (for example, appropriate GOSIP subprofiles).

11.6.3 Desirable requirements

The method of compliance to desirable requirements should be stated, and any requirements not being met should be clearly indicated.

To assist suppliers and avoid any omissions, the OR may include a statement of compliance that lists or references each mandatory and desirable requirement for the supplier to accept or reject.

11.6.4 Description of proposed infrastructure

The supplier must describe in detail the approach and proposed solution, and explain its benefits. Any restrictions and environmental requirements should be included. The description must include details of cable media (for example, type, number of cores, size, weight, bend radii), flexibility (for example, location and number of patches) and types of connection (at end equipment and for patching). Schematic diagrams should be provided by the supplier to assist in evaluation.

11.6.5 Timetables

The suppliers should be asked to illustrate how the timetable for procurement and implementation will be met. Lead times and installation times should be provided for each item, and any dates that the supplier views as critical if the programme is to be maintained should be stated - for example, latest contract award date.

11.6.6 Hardware configuration

The supplier should list the hardware components of the proposed solution, giving model numbers and descriptions. A functional schematic diagram of the infrastructure and the names of original manufacturers and countries of origin of the components should be provided.

11.6.7 Software and availability

Supply and maintenance details of any proposed software - for example, for active components or cable management - must be provided.

11.6.8 Maturity

The specifier should request details of product maturity for hardware and software - for example, date of first delivery, installed base and planned life of each element of the infrastructure.

11.6.9 Software packages

The supplier should give a view on the use of third-party software packages, and indicate the support they would offer. Examples would be cable management packages, which the organization may already use or may procure from elsewhere (unless the OR specifies those that the organization has already decided to use).

11.6.10 Loading/ sizing summary

The supplier should be asked to state what equipment they plan to install in each communications room or cable route. For example:

* space requirements
* equipment weights
* whether the large components may be dismantled for ease of handling

Section 11
The structure of the Operational Requirement

* how the equipment will be laid out
* access requirements
* power requirements
* heat output
* provision for future expansion.

11.6.11 Serviceability/reliability

The supplier must be asked to describe how the required availability is met, in terms of serviceability and reliability, and how the degree of resilience within the proposed infrastructure meets the requirements of the organization's Service Level Requirement (SLR).

11.6.12 Supporting services

The supplier should give details of maintenance services, training facilities, manuals and support personnel to be provided.

11.6.13 Costs

So that the project team can decide whether a proposal is likely to fall within the cost limits set, it is important that the supplier is asked to provide a summary of all relevant costs and to indicate the costs of any options offered. It will assist evaluation if the costs are grouped into the logical elements of the infrastructure, and if the figures enable variances to be calculated by the team. For example, costs should be presented for the cable backbone, local cable, hardware, installation, commissioning and management.

11.6.14 Further information

This section provides the suppliers with an opportunity to raise any outstanding points relating to the OR, to comment on features not specified in the OR, and to indicate why they should be selected to receive an invitation to tender.

11.7 Related guides

The sections above are provided to act as a reminder to the specifier of a cable infrastructure of the requirements for ORs. However, both the procurement process and the OR itself require detailed knowledge, and the specifier is referred to IS Guide B5, **The Operational Requirement**, and IS Guide B6, **Procurement**, which provide additional information.

The IT Infrastructure Library
Specification and Management of a Cable Infrastructure

Section 12
Evaluation

12. Evaluation

12.1 Obtaining value for money requires evaluation

The aim of evaluation

The main aim of evaluation, as for the Operational Requirement (OR), is to ensure that the organization obtains the best value from the money spent on a cable infrastructure.

The term best value does not mean the same as lowest tender price. The ability to meet both the short-term and longer-term requirements of the organization will be reflected in the cost, which may justify the acceptance of an offer that is not the lowest tender price.

This section of the module provides an overview of evaluation, with particular reference to the evaluation of responses to the OR for a cable infrastructure. Detailed guidance on evaluation will be found in the IS Guide B7, **Evaluation**.

12.2 Planning the evaluation process

12.2.1 When is evaluation required?

Evaluation needs to be considered on each occasion when a choice has to be made, from defining the scope and objectives of a project through to the post-implementation review. In the context of this module, the most important requirement for formal evaluation is during procurement, when it is applied to:

* shortlisting the potential supplier(s)
* evaluating tenders.

12.2.2 Developing the evaluation model

One of the benefits of a formal OR procedure is that it can provide a basis for evaluating proposals and selecting a shortlist of potential suppliers. The OR sets out a series of mandatory and desirable requirements - for example, quantification, standards and project management - and clearly these will form the basis of evaluation.

While these requirements are being prepared for the OR, the specifier should also be:

* preparing a document setting out the evaluation process
* developing the evaluation model to be used.

The evaluation model will list the requirements, and provide a space alongside to note the compliance offered by each supplier (that is, full, part, none). It will also include factors that are not mandatory or desirable in the OR, but that are important in selection - for example, the status of the supplier (see Section 12.3.2).

It is vital that the OR and evaluation criteria are complementary; otherwise, it is unlikely that the best, or even a viable, solution will be achieved. The content of the OR should be referenced when writing the evaluation model.

12.3 Evaluation criteria

Once the initial evaluation criteria have been used to shortlist suppliers and before a Memorandum of Agreement (MoA) is produced, the criteria should be refined and finalized. The finalized criteria will then be applied to tenders received from suppliers, and a contract will be awarded.

12.3.1 Selecting evaluation criteria

Tenders must be evaluated against a fixed set of criteria to ensure fair play and avoid bias. The criteria must be comprehensive and chosen to bring out the strengths and weaknesses of the tenders.

In general, the best way of developing the criteria is to begin with a checklist of broad headings that cover all the aspects of the project where potential criteria are expected to exist - for example, by using the shortlisting model.

The criteria are then built up by noting more specific details under each heading, as illustrated below. The final stage is to reach specific criteria, by including the mandatory and desirable requirements from the OR.

Section 12
Evaluation

12.3.2 Typical framework for evaluation criteria

A typical framework for evaluation criteria will consist of a series of major topics, each comprising a number of sub-topics. An example of such a framework follows, although the specifier should look for other topics and sub-topics relevant to the project in hand:

Degree of fit with OR
* ability to meet mandatory requirements from the OR
* degree of support of desirable requirements from the OR
* scope for additional value above minimum requirements

Status of supplier
* record (similar projects completed, experience)
* financial strength of company
* production capacity
* technical design capability
* quality assurance status
* variation management arrangements
* delivery capability
* after sales support and maintenance facilities (on site and at the factory)

Products
* conformance to required standards
* compatibility with existing systems (cable types, connectors)
* expansibility and adaptability of proposed products
* serviceability and reliability record
* maintainability and repair/servicing arrangements and options
* upgrade path and supplier's declared product development strategy (to emerging standards such as 10baseF and FDDI)
* replacement time frame
* availability and lead time of spares.

Implementation & support
* operational/financial effects of support required from the purchaser (office space, storage, telephone, FAX and so on)
* delivery and implementation flexibility (ability to reschedule and vary resources applied)
* quality of project management (for example, tools used, staff experience)
* quality of support arrangements
* provision of training, consultancy and other services.

Operational issues
* responsibilities to be borne by the organization
* number of subcontractors or third parties to be involved
* possibility of skills transfer to the organization.

Costs of acquisition
* tendered prices and NPV (see 12.5.2)
* likely costs of associated or follow-on orders
* payment terms (COD or progress/stage payments)
* discount options (for example, early payment terms)
* foreign exchange risks and costs
* price-variation arrangements between placing of contract and project completion (inflation clauses).

Operating costs
* maintenance costs
* warranties and technical guarantees offered
* administrative costs of supplier's procedures (for example, cable management package)
* staff training costs and necessary equipment
* cost of ongoing management, such as staff, tools, licences.

It is important to realize that some of these topics have a subjective element. The organization must use experience to assess priorities for each project, and adapt the basic criteria accordingly.

Section 12
Evaluation

12.3.3 Using the evaluation criteria

The evaluation criteria enable costs and benefits to be attributed to the tendered cable infrastructure solutions and any impact those solutions may have on the organization (for example, additional work services). Once all of the tenders have been evaluated, a comparison of costs and benefits is made to determine the solution which provides the best value.

12.4 Shortlisting

Once proposals have been received in response to the OR, the organization must shortlist suitable suppliers and proceed to further discussion.

Aims

The three aims of shortlisting are:

* to reduce the number of suppliers being considered, in order to make the procurement process more manageable, and in order to reduce costs to the organization and suppliers

* to ensure that shortlisted suppliers are able to provide an acceptable solution

* to stimulate vigorous competition between the shortlisted suppliers.

Considerations

Selection to the shortlist will typically be based on the following considerations:

* How well the proposal meets the mandatory requirements set out in the OR. Failure to satisfy all or part of any mandatory requirement will preclude further consideration of a proposal

* The degree to which the proposal meets the desirable requirements of the OR.

* The confidence that the organization has in the ability of the prospective supplier to complete the project successfully.

Essentially, shortlisting is about the quality of the technical solution offered, and confidence in the ability of the supplier to deliver. Price is a secondary consideration at this stage.

Many suppliers will offer a visit to a reference site as part of their response, and these can be a valuable way of assessing the ability to provide a quality solution. The visit should provide an opportunity to look at the quality of the installation, particularly the neatness of cabling and cross connects and to question the specifiers and managers of the infrastructure.

The shortlist should consist of between two and five suppliers; three is often considered an ideal number. If only one or two suppliers can meet the requirements, then the OR may need to be re-examined; perhaps the mandatory requirements are too restrictive, and could be amended and re-issued in a new OR.

A full explanation of shortlisting methods, including a recommended approach, can be found in IS Guide B7, **Evaluation**.

12.5 Evaluating tenders

12.5.1 Costs and benefits

The eventual aim of the process of refining the initial framework is to arrive at a final set of criteria that are defined precisely enough to enable financial costs or benefits to be calculated against each criterion. For example, it may be necessary for an organization to undertake environmental modifications or works services (such as larger risers and raised floors) to accommodate suppliers' proposed solutions. In such cases, the evaluation team will need to estimate the costs of these items for each supplier, and add them to the tendered costs.

A potential problem is that the value of a requirement may be less than the cost of providing it. To avoid the need to reveal the benefit values to suppliers, these situations should be anticipated by asking suppliers to provide the cost of the requirement as an option. If the cost of the option exceeds the value of the benefit, the option should be rejected. Typically, this could be applied to the provision of redundant components or convenience features.

If a tender does not meet a desirable requirement, then the value of that requirement should be added, as a cost penalty, to that supplier's tendered costs.

Financial values associated with evaluation criteria are termed attributed costs and benefits.

Section 12
Evaluation

12.5.2 Net present value

During evaluation of tenders, the attributed costs and benefits associated with each evaluation criterion are combined with the tendered costs, for each supplier, into a cash flow projection over the life of the infrastructure. Discounted cash flow techniques are then used to determine the net present value (NPV) of each solution. This enables a fair evaluation to be made of proposals that contain deferred expenditure. For example, the use of NPV allows a comparison to be made between the implementation of blown fibre (where the fibre cost is deferred) and conventional fibre-optic cable. Details of evaluation techniques are given in, **Investment Appraisal in the Public Sector: A Technical Guide for Government Departments**.

12.5.3 Spreadsheet modeling

The appraisal may use a simple pro-forma table, or may be produced using a computer spreadsheet to handle the calculations. The use of a spreadsheet is particularly helpful for modelling the effects of changes - for example, the number of occupants of a building may have been unknown at the time of tendering, and a best estimate may have been included in the ITT for user-dependent items such as fibre-optic interfaces and patch cords. Provided that suppliers have quoted unit prices, the model can be used to obtain a range of costs for each supplier - for example, for high, medium and low occupancy, over a range of timescales - and can also reveal any step changes in costs as, for example, the number of services or connections increases. This process is known as sensitivity analysis, and can provide useful information, particularly of the longer-term costs of a proposal. However, the analysis is subjective and should be treated as an unquantifiable factor in the final decision.

12.5.4 Unquantifiable factors

The objective of setting evaluation criteria is to make all the factors quantifiable. However, some aspects, such as a supplier's understanding of strategic cabling, can be judged only against experience. Visits to reference sites and factories provide a valuable opportunity to assess these areas, and should be taken up - quality of workmanship can be examined and an impression formed of the general attitude and ability of the supplier and its staff.

The IT Infrastructure Library
Specification and Management of a Cable Infrastructure

Great care must be taken, however, to ensure that subjective, unquantifiable factors do not replace objective factors in the evaluation and that, wherever possible, they are addressed before shortlisting.

Single tender evaluation   Should only one acceptable tender be received, it must still be evaluated formally to calculate the life cost of the proposal, including attributed costs. This procedure is necessary to ensure that the tender falls within the original financial approval given for the project.

12.5.5 Evaluation report

At the end of evaluation, an evaluation report must be produced. The purposes of this report are to:

* recommend the most appropriate supplier(s) for the project

* describe the way in which the evaluation has been conducted

* relate the evaluation objectives to those of the project

* provide the key facts and assessments supporting the recommendation

* present the total cost of the recommended solution.

The report should be written, so far as is possible in non-technical language, and should include a full description of the evaluation model and criteria, together with the results of the investment appraisal. Any use of unquantifiable factors during the tender evaluation should also be described.

Section 13
Commissioning and acceptance testing

13. Commissioning and acceptance testing

13.1 Why, who and when?

Purpose of testing

Commissioning and acceptance tests are required to verify that the cable infrastructure, as installed, meets the specification agreed between the supplier and the purchaser.

The proof is in the form of tests carried out both during and after the installation and the documented evidence of satisfactory results.

Procedures

The requirements for acceptance tests must be specified, or at least outlined, in the OR, to ensure that the test procedures are clearly understood before installation commences. In the case of a CC88 procurement, test conditions would normally be according to part 3A (Procedures for Trials of Information Technology Systems by the Authority Using a Workload), with extensive use being made of the facility to incorporate demonstrations. The cable management tool should be used to record the installation and acceptance of the cable infrastructure components.

Specifying and controlling tests

Although the onus is on the supplier to demonstrate that the implementation has been completed correctly, it is recommended that the purchaser should take an active role in the specification and control of the test procedures. This approach is particularly important when integrating with existing products where, without clear statements of responsibility and careful management, the natural tendency of suppliers to blame each other for failures will prevail.

The management of testing places a further burden on the project team in the form of manpower and project timescale, but is a vital element of a cable infrastructure project.

Carrying out tests

The Operational Requirement (OR) should state that commissioning and acceptance testing will be carried out by the supplier and witnessed by the purchaser. (The purchaser's representative must be a competent person - that is, one who understands the purpose, method and results of the tests.)

There will be exceptions when it is not possible for the suppliers to carry out the tests, and the purchaser must carry them out. Examples would be testing delivery of a service not available at the time of the installation, or for

The IT Infrastructure Library
Specification and Management of a Cable Infrastructure

reasons of security. These situations will usually be known in advance of the installation, and the specifier of the infrastructure should make any unusual requirements or constraints clear in the OR and subsequent contractual documentation.

Timing of test

Commissioning and acceptance tests must not be left until the installation is entirely complete - many should be part of the ongoing management of the implementation. For example, incorrectly routed or labelled cables will be much easier to detect - and correct - before they are buried beneath others.

Some tests may also be specified to take place a considerable time after the installation is complete. For example, tests to ensure that there has been no degradation in performance may be specified, typically 12 months after completion of the installation phase.

The organization has the ultimate responsibility to take title to the infrastructure and complete the contract by formal acceptance. Any tests including live running must be agreed in advance by inclusion in contracts; the infrastructure must not be simply put into use as this could imply acceptance.

13.2 Details of the test procedure

The test procedure should include details of:

* the tests required
* the test methods (that is, the way the tests are to be conducted)
* the test acceptance criteria
* the format of the results (for example, tables, graphs and so on).

It is necessary to describe (if not specify precisely) the acceptance test requirements in the MoA and ITT so that the supplier can bid appropriate resources and costs.

Safety

Regulations such as the Health and Safety at Work Act 1974 place responsibilities on the organization and its agents. These aspects are not dealt with in this module.

Section 13
Commissioning and acceptance testing

Avoid Ambiguity
For the test results to be of benefit, it is essential that the tests required are not ambiguous and that they have a clear outcome. The criteria for pass and fail must therefore be clearly specified, without leaving scope for misinterpretation.

Logical order
To help the project manager and suppliers to follow the procedures, and so to help ensure that the tests are carried out correctly, tests should be specified in a logical order and a programme produced to specify when the tests are to be carried out. Drawing a flow chart of the procedures may assist the specifier in producing a clear, logical progression.

Test methods
Each test should have a documented method, including the criteria for pass and fail and the action to be taken in each case. This method must be adhered to, and the project manager should ensure that it is followed.

Documented results
Every result from a test, or from a part of a test, must be recorded immediately as a pass or fail, irrespective of whether the test is carried out as part of commissioning or final acceptance. Documentation is important since it allows later analysis of test results and enables tests to be repeated where results are in question. The project manager should obtain all the result sheets from the suppliers, include them in the infrastructure documentation and update the configuration database records including the cable management tool.

Incident log
In addition to the fail on the record sheet, a test failure should also be recorded in an incident log detailing the test, the item(s) tested, the time and date of the test, the nature of the incident (symptom and cause) and the corrective action taken. This log provides a useful reference when diagnosing operational problems, and will reveal patterns in the occurrence of incidents, and should be specified as a contractual requirement.

A record should also be kept of equipment failures to enable rogue units or products to be identified.

13.3 Details of the tests

A layered approach
When specifying a test procedure, it may be helpful to consider the infrastructure as a number of layers, and to develop the procedure layer by layer.

121

The IT Infrastructure Library
Specification and Management of a Cable Infrastructure

For example, three layers in a cable infrastructure could be visualized as being:

* physical (for example, cables, cross connects, cabinets)
* link (for example, transceivers, multiple access units (MAUs), fibre-optic interfaces)
* network (for example, user configuration, applications).

Each of these levels, although not independent, will need to have a set of tests specified.

Physical tests

The objective of the physical tests is to ensure that:

* the correct components have been supplied
* components are installed correctly
* components are in the right location
* documentation is accurate and complete.

The tests specified for the physical level of the infrastructure should include, but may not be limited to:

* safety tests - for example, of earthing, fuses, circuit breakers, earth loop impedance and cable insulation

  (It is usual to ask suppliers to certify that these tests have been carried out as part of commissioning)

* checks on cable types, quantities, routes, labels
* visual checks of equipment - for example, model, quantity, options, location, fixing
* inspection of installation workmanship and adherence to specification
* preconnection inspection (PCI) for voice cabling and the PABX (required for connection to be made to the public network and detailed in CC88 Part 3-D: **Procedures for Trials of PBX systems**)
* continuity tests for copper cables and attenuation tests for fibre-optic cables
* examination and checks on documentation and records
* checks on conformance to the specified standards.

Section 13
Commissioning and acceptance testing

Link tests

The link tests should be specified to ensure that the components in the infrastructure operate correctly, when taken in isolation from other elements. Tests will include:

* testing of active components in the cabling - for example, fibre-optic interfaces, transceivers, multiplexors, modems, bridges, gateways

* connecting a terminal and file server over the cabling, and checking that a log on can be achieved.

These tests will often be bit error-rate tests - the transmission of data over a link while monitoring the output for errors. These tests should be carried out over a wide range of transmission speeds to test the equipment fully.

The specifier must also attempt to ensure that communication tests are sufficiently rigorous to detect equipment not performing to specification. A suitable procedure would usually require tests to be an order of magnitude greater than the acceptable error rates. For example, a product with a specified bit error rate of 1 in 10^9 should be tested with 10^{10} bits (an order of magnitude greater). That may result in lengthy tests that cannot be accommodated within the test programme. At a bit rate of 19,200 bits per second, the test would take 144 hours to complete, which may not be practical. Acceptance would then depend on satisfactory operational performance. If this is the case, final acceptance should be conditional on satisfactory performance over a longer, operational period to avoid the risks of not detecting faults during short tests.

Network tests

The objective of the network tests is to confirm that the logical topology is correctly configured, and that services more complex than point-to-point are supported correctly. These tests will involve the simulation or operation of local area networks, and may include testing connections into wide area networks.

Usually, the organization will need to draw upon its own networking staff, or seek external specialist assistance such as third-party independent test organizations, to specify and carry out these tests, supported by the supplier as necessary.

Failures

If a test results in a failure, the fault should be logged (see section 13.2) and then repaired. Once the supplier has corrected the fault, the test should be repeated.

The IT Infrastructure Library
Specification and Management of a Cable Infrastructure

13.4 Sampling

When to use

To carry out the types of tests outlined above on all components of a cable infrastructure would be slow and expensive. With the exception of safety tests, a compromise is usually adopted, where only a sample of each component is tested. The sample chosen should be sufficiently large to be representative - an order of magnitude above the expected fault rate is accepted practice.

For example, although all components must be tested for safety, typically only 10 per cent of the patch connections need to be checked initially against the records.

Increasing the sample size

If a fault is recorded from the sample taken, the test should be repeated, preferably on a larger sample, to quantify the problem. Once the supplier considers that the faults have been rectified, a new sample should be tested to confirm that the work is carried out correctly. The initial sampling levels, and the escalation, should be included in the specification of each test.

Section 14
Standards

14. Standards

14.1 The use of standards

The specification of a cable infrastructure will be influenced in many ways by standards - more accurately, by Standards, regulations and guidelines - which are often interrelated.

To a specifier only partially familiar with standards, their use may appear initially to be a constraint on the infrastructure specification. Cable media are restricted, and cable lengths limited. However, standards provide significant benefits to a specifier who is familiar with their content and uses them constructively. For example:

* a Standards-compliant cable infrastructure should be safe (IEE wiring regulations)

* a Standards-based infrastructure helps to ensure product compatibility between suppliers' equipment

* the specifier can be confident that the infrastructure will be able to support a wide a variety of strategic services

* the specifier is freed from unnecessary detail - for example, by referencing a Standard rather than including detailed methods of installation or technical specification (for example, BS6701)

* reference to Standards makes specification easier and conformance verifiable.

Care must be taken in the use of Standards, to ensure that they do not control the specification. Standards do not always provide unique solutions, and must not be used as a substitute for a proper specification process. Although standards are not a panacea, the benefits of a standards-based specification are considerable and the adoption of Standards, guides and regulations is essential for strategic cabling.

14.2 Sources of Standards, guides and regulations

Standards, guides and regulations can be grouped conveniently into four categories:

* international
* national

* draft (or emerging)
* *de facto*.

Each of these groups is examined below, listing the standards that the specifier may wish to reference, or may be referred to by third parties.

14.3 International Standards, guides and regulations

International standards, guides and regulations relevant to strategic cabling originate from organizations in the US and Europe, such as:

* CCITT International Consultative Committee for Telegraphy and Telecommunications
* CEN/CENELEC European Committee for Standardization
* EIA/TIA Electrical Industries Association/ Telecommunications Industries Association (North America)
* IEEE Institution of Electrical and Electronic Engineers (US)
* ISO International Standards Organization
* IEC International Electrotechnical Commission
* EC European Council.

Standards relevant to the specification of an infrastructure, at the time of writing are:

EC 87/95	Council decision; standardization in the field of IT and telecommunications (open systems).
EC 89/336	EC directive on electromagnetic compatibility (mandatory from 1 January 1992).
IEC 332-3	Tests on bunched cables. Test specification for spread of fire along cables.
IEC 847	Characteristics of LANs, 1988. (Equivalent to BS 89/65578)
IEEE 802.3, 802.5	LAN standards; CSMA/CD and Token Ring.
ISO 8802/3, 8802/5	LAN standards; CSMA/CD and Token Ring (equivalent to IEEE 802.3, 802.5).
ISO 8877	Specification of an 8-wire data jack (RJ45)

Section 14
Standards

ISO 9000	see BS 5750 (National standards)
UL	Underwriters laboratory. US approvals board, covering electrical safety and fire specifications.

14.4 National Standards, guides and regulations

14.4.1 Standards

National Standards relevant to strategic cabling originate from the BSI (British Standards Institution) and apply to many aspects of strategic cabling. Those relevant at the time of writing are:

BS 6701 — Code of practice for installation of apparatus intended for connection to certain telecommunications systems; also applicable to data, especially for UTP (supersedes the previous BS 6506)

    Part 1 — General recommendations. (1986).

    Part 2 — Installation of switching apparatus that may be connected to certain analogue telecommunications systems. (1987).

BS 8877 — Specification for an 8-wire data plug and socket; (RJ-45).

BS 6312 — Specification for a national standard telephone jack; the LJU-6.

BS 5750 — Quality assurance standard.

BS 5839 — Parts 1 and 2; specification for the use of telecommunications services to run fire alarms. Fire alarm cables to be dedicated - that is, not shared by other services, voice or data.

14.4.2 Guides

GOSIP — Procurement guidance on open systems interconnection, including LANs.

NICEIC — National Inspection Council for Electrical Engineering Contractors; guidance for quality of electrical work.

14.4.3 Regulations

Building regulations 1985 — Requirements to control the spread of fires, including regulations for fire resistance of shafts (risers) and sealing of openings used for cable access.

Building (inner London) regulations	Section 20 applies where a building has a storey at a greater height than 30 metres (25m where the area of the building exceeds 930 m^2) or where a trade building has a volume of more than 7,100m^3. Section 20 conformance requires specialist consideration of fire protection, including the specification of any raised flooring, cable materials and fire breaks.
Regulations for electrical installations	Institution of Electrical Engineers. Non-statutory regulations relating principally to the design, selection, erection, inspection and testing of electrical installations.
Health and Safety at Work Act 1974	Regulations governing working practices at places of work.
Telecommunications Act 1984	Cabling attached to the public network must be maintained by the same contractor as telecommunications apparatus - who must be an approved maintenance authority.
Oftel	Regulations controlling the use of cable for voice and data, and of only BABT-approved products for connection to the public network.

14.5 Emerging standards

The growth in strategic cabling has stimulated activity by the standards bodies to produce standards specifically for cable infrastructures. Those under development at the time of writing, which are already influencing the specification of infrastructures are:

EIA PN 2072	Building standards for telecommunications media and systems.
EIA/TIA - 492	Generic specification for optical waveguide fibres. EIA, 1987. Useful when specifying FDDI compatible fibre, and referenced in Annex B.
EIA/TIA SP-1907	Commercial building wiring standard. The primary reference in Annex B.
EIA 569	Commercial building standard for telecommunications pathways and spaces.
ISO/JTC1/SC83/WG3	Generic cabling for customer premises. Study aligned with EIA/TIA 1907.
BS 89/65578 DC	Draft standard on specification for the characteristics of local area networks.
IEEE 802	Guidance for the implementation of local area networks.

BSI IST 6/10/1	A cable installation practice standard is being developed by a BSI working group.
FDDI	Fibre distributed data interface. A 100M bit/s token passing ring network using fibre-optics for the ring cabling.

14.6 *De facto* **standards**

Manufacturers have often attempted to produce proprietary, *de facto*, standards to promote sales and lock customers into their own products. However, many originally proprietary standards are now supported by national and international Standards (for example, Token Ring and Ethernet). Some *de facto* standards will also be produced by industry organizations.

The specifier of a cable infrastructure should avoid *de facto* standards that are not supported by ratified standards, thus avoiding restrictions on flexibility. *De facto* standards are not usually as stable as ratified standards.

The IT Infrastructure Library
Specification and Management of a Cable Infrastructure

15. Management of the installation of cables

15.1 Installation management must be carefully planned

For the installation of a cable infrastructure to be a success, it must be planned and managed with considerable care and attention to detail. Careful planning reduces the risk of unforeseen problems jeopardizing the overall critical success factors of quality, cost and time.

A number of the areas to be planned are the subject of separate sections of this module (for example, commissioning and acceptance testing which is discussed in section 13). The focus of this section is on planning the installation of the infrastructure and ensuring the essential co-ordination with other on-site activities, both when developing the plans and also on an ongoing basis. Failure to co-ordinate plans may result in costly delays. Planning will involve the client, contractor, quantity surveyor and developer.

Examples of factors to be considered in the planning of an implementation are:

* delivery to site (for example, restriction on size of vehicle, delivery hours, co-ordination, goods received signatory)

* secure storage on-site or off-site for tools and components

* availability of power and adequate lighting when required

* on-site project management procedures (a decision taken quickly on the spot by an authorized person, often avoids lengthy communications)

* removal of refuse, such as old cables and packaging

* integration of works services and cable infrastructure activities.

The last item, integration of activities, often has two facets.

These are:

* co-ordination with non-IT fitting-out trades (plastering, flooring, ceilings, partitioning) and electrical works

* sequencing implementation throughout the building.

Co-ordination and sequencing are essential management aspects of a cable infrastructure implementation project.

15.2 Co-ordination with fitting out

Whether the cable infrastructure is installed as part of a new building project, a redevelopment or a refurbishment, it is likely that there will be other, non-IT, fitting-out tasks to be undertaken. Integration of the IT fit-out with the building fit-out programme is recommended since it provides opportunities for significant cost and time savings to be made. When this integration cannot be achieved, installation of the cable infrastructure could be left until the other trades are off-site, but the opportunities mentioned above will be lost.

An example of the benefits of integration is the ease of access to underfloor cable routes. Lifting floor tiles to cable beneath a raised floor is quicker and easier before the floor finishes are laid. Raising clear runs of tiles for cabling once partitioning is in place is often difficult, and may even require partitions to be removed.

Although every infrastructure project will have a different set of constraints on the programme, co-ordination plans will often be similar. An example is shown in figure 29, where typical activities are listed; each activity would be the subject of a detailed planning and co-ordination sub-project. For example, the cabling element could include:

* removal of old cables

* installation of horizontal cables

* installation of backbone cables

* termination (copper)

* patching

* configuration

* acceptance testing.

Section 15
Management of the installation of cables

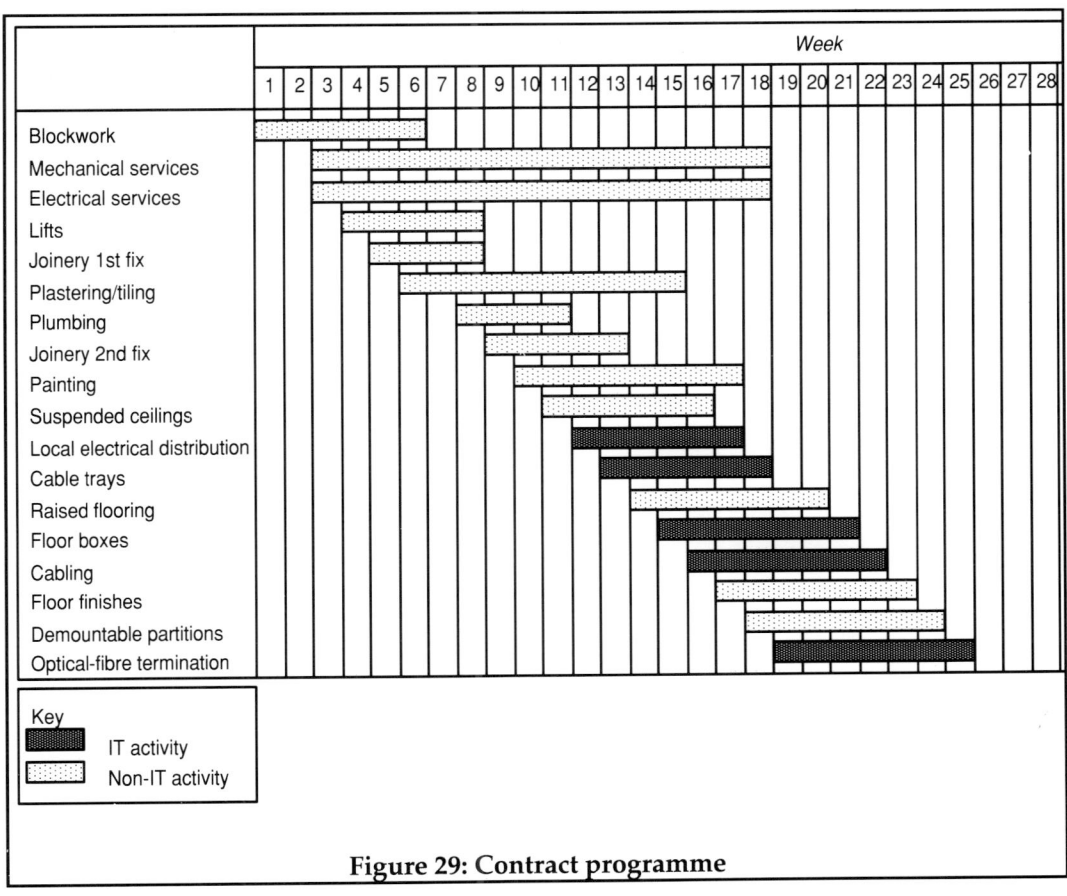

Figure 29: Contract programme

The implementation programme must be developed with the co-operation of the main fitting-out contractor who will need to grant access to the site for craftsmen, under an 'Artisans and tradesmen agreement', if the IT installation is not carried out by the main contractor.

Figure 30, overleaf, illustrates the same notional project as figure 29 but with IT implementation carried out after the main contractor has finished fit-out. Tasks take longer for the reasons outlined above, and the project duration increases from 25 to 36 weeks.

The IT Infrastructure Library
Specification and Management of a Cable Infrastructure

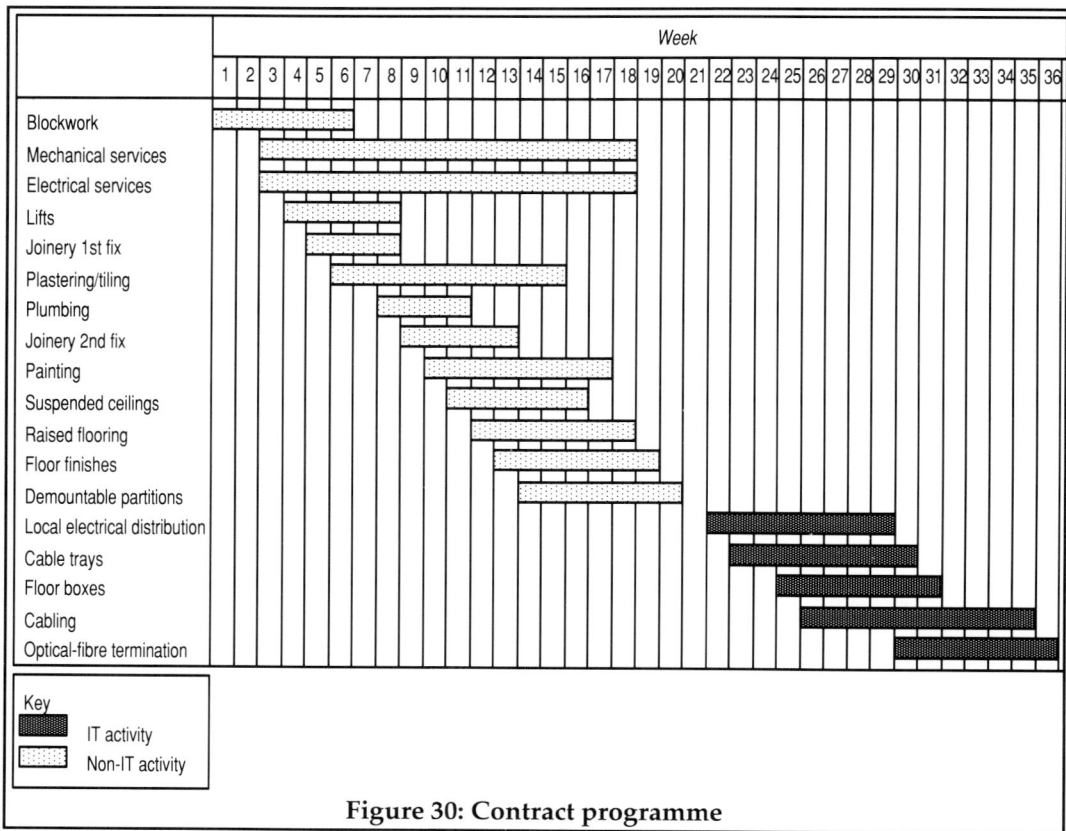

Figure 30: Contract programme

15.3 Sequencing installation

Many developments are fitted out on a top-down basis. The upper floors are fitted out first, and the finishing trades then progress down the building. In general, this is not a constraint on the IT installation, as strategic cabling is easily installed on a floor-by-floor basis. However, there are potential problems, and the Cabling Manager should be involved as early as possible in the fitting-out sequencing to avoid unnecessary delays. For example:

* fitting out of network, PABX and frame rooms - often in the lower part of the building - may need to be promoted in the schedule to allow early access for cabling and installation of equipment

* access to risers is required from each floor if backbone cabling is to be installed continuously and not to each floor sequentially

* HVAC installations in areas such as the PABX room or computer suite must be commissioned before IT equipment is installed to avoid dirt being blown into the equipment and to provide necessary cooling during acceptance and commissioning tests.

When possible, the ITT issued in the selection of the main contractor for a development should clearly state that a cable infrastructure is to be installed and describe the scope of the work. The developer must expect to be required to co-operate with the Cabling Manager in planning the detail of fitting out, to allow access to site for surveys, and to provide access for craftsmen.

15.4 Timescales

The time taken to specify, install and commission a cable infrastructure depends on a large number of variables, including the organization's experience, the complexity of the infrastructure and the time and resources available.

Two factors are important:

* the time and resources required for planning should not be underestimated

* the earlier the IT team is involved in planning the project the more effectively it will be able to combine the IT fit-out with the building programme.

Typical durations for cable infrastructure projects, from conception to completion are:

* 4,000m^2 redevelopment   6-9 months

* 10,000m^2 development   6-12months.

But it is possible to complete implementations more quickly - for example, on subsequent projects when procedures do not need to be reinvented or by engaging external assistance.

The IT Infrastructure Library
Specification and Management of a Cable Infrastructure

Section 16
Cable management tools

16. Cable management tools

16.1 The need for cable management tools

The objective of strategic cabling is to install an infrastructure that will support changing requirements of end users. Cabling is a fundamental element of the IT infrastructure, and its management must be an integral part of the total infrastructure management including configuration, problem and change management. Cable management tools provide a mechanism for planning, recording, and controlling all changes to the infrastructure. Throughout the life of the cable infrastructure, and in particular, during the first year after installation, office layouts will change and staff will move around the building, so the organization will need to make frequent changes to the patching. As different logical topologies are adopted, it is important not just to support them, but also to manage the different rates of change within the infrastructure.

Accurate record keeping throughout these reconfigurations is essential. Indeed, keeping accurate records of PABX wiring is a requirement of the Branch Systems General Licence (BSGL). However, it is essential that the management tools are in place before cables are installed, so that details can be entered as cables are installed.

16.2 What tools are available?

There are three broad categories of cable management tools available to support the management of cable infrastructures in different sized buildings (or parts of multi-tenanted buildings). It is important that an appropriate tool for the management task in hand is selected, particularly for large installations. The specifier should also ensure that the cable management tool can be integrated into any existing configuration management tools and procedures used.

The three categories of tools, with typical net lettable areas (NLAs) and staff numbers for which they are appropriate are:

* paper-based records (small offices - say, up to 1,000m^2 or 100 staff)

The IT Infrastructure Library
Specification and Management of a Cable Infrastructure

* automated records (medium sized offices - up to 10,000m^2 or 1,000 staff)

* automated records, integrated with drawings (large offices - say, over 10,000m^2 or 1,000 staff).

If the records of a number of offices are to be centralized, then the total office size or number of staff should be used. These packages are discussed below, and the resources required are discussed in section 16.3.

16.2.1 Paper records

For a small cable infrastructure, keeping paper records may be the most convenient and cost-effective option and requires no expenditure on hardware. Suitable documentation to tabulate the data is available commercially in preprinted forms, or can be devised by the organization. Cable routes and equipment layouts can be marked up on paper drawings of the building. Should the records be destroyed, then a full audit would be feasible, and could be undertaken to restore them. However, it is recommended that a duplicate set of records be maintained in contingency planning procedures. These records may be kept off-site, in a fireproof safe, or in another suitable location.

Although easy to set up, paper records are difficult to change, and can be difficult to cross-reference.

16.2.2 Automated records for medium sized offices

A medium sized cable infrastructure, say 5,000m^2 of NLA, would typically require records to be kept of between 2,500 and 4,000 cables in the local distribution plus backbone cables and the patching configuration. A typical number of occupants - say 500 - is also likely to generate between 100 and 200 change requests per annum, possibly greater in the early months after occupation.

For the effective management of the information, the records should be kept on a personal or portable computer with a card index file package. Automation avoids large numbers of paper records and enables data to be sorted, accessed and changed more quickly - for example, by end equipment, cable number, patch connection or host computer port.

Section 16
Cable management tools

The software functions required for simple automated records are available from many common database and spreadsheet packages, and although training will be necessary, specialist computing skills will not usually be required. Drawings need not be computerized: numbering systematically the presentations and marking cable routes onto paper drawings should provide an adequate reference for use alongside the automated records.

16.2.3 Automated records for large offices

The demands made of cable management in a large building or group of buildings are often disproportionately greater than for smaller offices. Not only has a larger volume of information to be recorded but management is more complex, procedures will be more elaborate and more staff will be involved. For example, in a small or medium sized building, the Cable Manager can easily record requested changes and personally update the records once they have been carried out - often by the manager in person. A large infrastructure may have many change requests outstanding at any one time, and changes are less likely to be implemented by the Cable Manager. A large cable infrastructure is also likely to include a greater diversity of cable and equipment types than a smaller one - again adding to the complexity of the records.

These requirements place a greater emphasis on the need to control change, not merely to maintain records, and for features more advanced than those found on database or spreadsheet software. For example, the software should be able to generate drawings and a list of all the changes needed to achieve a specific result such as relocating a business group to a new location in the building.

Many additional benefits can be gained from the use of specialized cable management tools - for example, the ability to:

* raise a caution if cable routes are filled or loaded to pre-set limits

* ensure that standards are followed, for example by warning if permitted cable lengths are exceeded

* generate work orders for changes

* flag configuration database items (CDBI) which are subject to an outstanding change request

* represent any circuit graphically, indicating user, equipment, cable numbers and patching configuration
* interface with computer-aided design (CAD) facilities.

A CAD package can be used as a design tool for the cabling and to avoid lengthy data input. Architects' drawings are loaded from disc or by scanning, and building information is built up in a series of 'layers' onto the drawing (structural grid, walls, floor tile grid, cable routes and so on). Cable routes and equipment are drawn on screen, and the records database is compiled automatically. In addition, the tools may be able to produce cable installation schedules as shown in figure 31. Changes can be made on the drawings to cables or routes, and the database will update automatically.

Cable no. (a)	From (b)	To (c)	Type (d)	Length (e)	Installer (f)	Status (g)	Route (h)
B-NS-C-1001	HO-001-B-137-2	B-NS-M-198	AA	81 m	BT	2	123-124,
							124-125,
							125-126,
							126-127

a   cable number (see section 4: Cable Infrastructure management)
b   start equipment or connection number
c   end equipment or connection number
d   cable type code, for example AA = 4pr UTP
e   automatically calculated length
f   responsibility
g   for example,
       0 = not installed
       1 = installed, not accepted
       2 = accepted, not in use
       3 = in use
h   route shown as sequence of route segments, set up during the design

Figure 31: Typical CAD generated cable schedule

Section 16
Cable management tools

A CAD-based cable management tool can be used for other, related, tasks. For example:

* inventory control; displaying details of equipment picked out from an on-screen drawing
* space planning; designing layouts and reorganizations.

The use of a CAD tool may require an operator who is skilled in the CAD package used. Emerging products may require fewer skills, typically by a greater use of pull-down menus and commands in English. However, the operator must still be computer-literate, and have a good understanding of cable management. Current CAD tools are not suitable for operation by clerical staff.

16.3 Resources

There are two resources required for cable management tools, namely people and hardware (computer or pro-formas). It is essential that the tool, no matter how simple or complex, is the responsibility of a single individual. This responsibility is designated to ensure that the tool is maintained and that changes are always entered. For a small installation, the effort required will be minimal; for a large infrastructure, control of changes may be a full-time position in the help desk function.

A computerized package may be single-user or multi-user. If multi-user, the person responsible for the tool should consider the levels of access allowed to other staff. For example, the Cable Manager may have access to effect major changes such as additions or deletions, technical support have access for changing patching; and other help desk personnel might have access on a read-only basis for 'what if' modelling.

There are several PC based cable management tools of varying sophistication, which will define their memory and graphics requirements. Some larger infrastructure packages will be multi-user CAD based, and will need to run on a minicomputer.

16.4 Limitations and costs

No cable management procedure will be successful unless information is accurate because no tool can compensate for errors or out-of-date information. The onus on the organization is to ensure that accurate records are taken of an installation, and subsequently maintained, irrespective of the tool being used. Back-up records are essential, either off-site or in a suitable location such as a fireproof safe.

Cable management tools are not generally integrated with network management systems, although this is not usually critical provided that common numbering schemes are adopted. Other limitations depend upon the package used. For example, it is often possible to enter impossible configurations into a design package - say, moving a presentation beyond the reach of its cables or joining incompatible connectors. The organization must therefore realize that the tools are an aid to, not a replacement for, management and design.

The cost of a cable management system varies according to the features it offers and the hardware required to operate it. Generally, however, a system for a medium sized building may cost (at the time of writing this module) between £5,000 and £15,000 and, for a large organization which may comprise many buildings, between £20,000 and £100,000 including hardware.

Cable management tools are essential elements of strategic cabling and are required if the flexibility of the cabling is to be both utilized and maintained. Resources such as hardware, software and manpower must be adequate to ensure effective maintenance of the cable infrastructure records. Inadequate resources will result in inaccurate records, which will not be conducive to effective cable management.

In order to incorporate the management of the cable infrastructure in that of the IT, the cable management tool should be an integral part of the organization's configuration, change and problem management. Current cable management tools offer very limited integration potential. However, there may be long term benefits, in terms of management costs, in investing in an adaptable tool.

17. Benefits, costs and possible problems

17.1 Benefits available

The benefits of adopting a strategic approach to cabling are set out in the IT Infrastructure Library module, **Cable Infrastructure Strategy**.

The main benefit to be gained from the quality specification and management of a cable infrastructure is that the organization's cabling strategy can be implemented in an efficient and cost-effective manner. This benefit is achieved by the ability to:

* provide flexibility without the costs of over-provision (quantification, topology)
* meet availability requirements without excessive costs (specification of reliability and resilience)
* support strategic communications standards and new local area networking technologies without recabling (specification of media)
* maintain flexibility throughout the life of the infrastructure irrespective of end-user moves and changes (management)
* ensure that suitable accommodation for IT is provided (liaison with other parties)
* ensure co-ordination within M & E Services to avoid conflicts in installation (installation management)
* implement the infrastructure in a timely, cost-effective manner (management and implementation).

In summary, the correct specification and management of a cable infrastructure will enable the financial benefits of strategic cabling to be fully realized and maintained throughout the life of the infrastructure, increasing the net present value (NPV) of the project and avoiding expensive mistakes.

17.2 The costs of specification and management

Specification

A good specification cannot be produced without adequate resources, or aspects will be rushed and, more seriously, overlooked, if the process is not to lengthen and delay the implementation. The main cost of specification is therefore the investment in time. An organization must budget many days of effort - typically between 50 and 100 - to cover the specification topics included or referenced in this module, and also to allow a sufficient period for the processes to be carried out.

Planning and specification of the cabling should commence at an early stage in the implementation of a strategic IT infrastructure. For example, it may be desirable to brief architects one or even two years before the first cables are installed to influence the design of a building to include sufficient risers of adequate size or adequate raised floors. It is also desirable to plan ahead for environmental services requirements, and to monitor emerging standards that may take two to three years to be ratified.

If the installation is into an existing building, resources will also be needed for assessing its suitability and to audit any existing cabling.

Management

Management of the implementation will require further resources to inspect, test and ensure compliance. Typically this resource will be a minimum of one day per week prior to installation and a minimum of one person available full-time once the installation is under way. Subsequent on-going management will also require resources - for example, for move and change. The resources required will be determined by the size of the infrastructure, the practices of the organization and the tools deployed.

Maintenance

Maintenance costs will be included as a part of the supplier-evaluation process, and would not usually be considered a specification or management cost.

Price of failure

Failing to specify and manage an infrastructure adequately can be very costly. The potential problems of a poor specification can easily be visualized as cabling unfit for its intended purpose, which may result in constraints on the business operation. Poor management can result in an infrastructure becoming obsolete long before the expiry of the payback period used to justify the investment. Once records are inaccurate, it is easier, in the short term, to lay new cable than to locate existing spare capacity - until cable routes fill up and the cabling must all be ripped out and replaced.

Section 17
Benefits, costs and possible problems

17.3 Possible problems

There are several problems that may be encountered during the specification and management of a cable infrastructure, and that must be overcome for a project to be successful. For example:

* senior management commitment and approval of the necessary resources may not be forthcoming

* if the IS strategy has to be revised, the infrastructure may not fully support the new strategic direction.

* control of the infrastructure is likely to be lost totally because of the late installation of suitable management tools, a failure to establish cable records during design and installation, or a failure to maintain them due to operational pressures

* external advisers may fail to understand the organization's needs fully and so provide inadequate guidance.

Strategic cabling can be a success only as part of an overall strategic approach to IT that also includes data communications. It cannot be undertaken successfully in isolation.

To obviate these potential problems, it is vital that an organization embarking on a cable infrastructure does so with full commitment to the project, and the necessary resources and experience both to carry it through to completion and to provide ongoing management. If this resource is not available within the organization, it should be bought in. The success of the project is, ultimately, dependent upon the commitment of the organization's senior management to strategic cabling. They must authorize the resources for the project and have ultimate accountability for its success or failure.

The IT Infrastructure Library
Specification and Management of a Cable Infrastructure

Section 18
Bibliography

18. Bibliography

18.1 CCTA

18.1.1 Information Systems (IS) Guides

A5. A Project Manager's Guide:
ISBN 0 471 92525 X.

B2. The Feasibility Study:
ISBN 0 471 92527 6.

B4. Appraising Investment in Information Systems:
ISBN 0 471 92529 2.

B5. The Operational Requirement:
ISBN 0 471 92530 6.

B6. Procurement:
ISBN 0 471 92531 4.

B7. Evaluation:
ISBN 0 471 92532 2.

18.1.2 Other CCTA publications

A Guide to System Reliability and Availability; 1988

ADEPT-2; 1991

CC88 - Rules for Tendering and General Conditions of Contract; 1988

Government Open Systems Interconnection Profile (GOSIP); Published by HMSO

The PRINCE project management methodology: an overview; 1990

Investment Appraisal in the Public Sector: A Technical Guide for Government Departments.

18.2 Other publications

18.2.1 Standards

Relevant standards are detailed in Section 14 of this module.

18.2.2 Books and journals

Communications Engineering International; April 1990 issue

Communications Infrastructure for Buildings; published by Butler Cox 1988

IEE Review; April 1990 issue

Information Technology and Buildings - A practical guide for designers; Butler Cox 1989

Local Computer Network Technologies; Academic Press 1981

The EOSYS Cabling Guide for Building Professionals; published by EOSYS 1988

Wiring up the Workplace; published by IBC Technical Services Ltd 1986.

Annex A. Glossary of terms

Acronyms and abbreviations used in this module

ADEPT-2	A Decision Environment for PRINCE Tasks
ANSI	American National Standards Institution
BABT	British Approvals Board for Telecommunications
BDF	Building distribution frame - the main patch facility
BSGL	Branch System General Licence
BSI	British Standards Institution
CAD	Computer Aided Design
CC88	CCTA Rules for Tendering and General Conditions of Contract
CPU	Central processing unit
CRAMM	CCTA Risk Analysis and Management Methodology
CSMA/CD	Carrier Sense Multiple Access/ Collision Detect
EIA/TIA	Electronic Industries Association/ Telecommunication Industries Association (North America)
EMI	Electromagnetic interference
FDDI	Fibre distributed data interface
FOIRL	Fibre-optic inter-repeater link
GOSIP	Government Open Systems Interconnection Profile
HVAC	Heating, ventilation and air conditioning
IDC	Insulation displacement connector
IEC	International Electrotechnical Commission
IEE	Institution of Electrical Engineers
IEEE	Institution of Electrical and Electronic Engineers (USA)
IS	Information System
ISDN	Integrated services digital network
ISO	International Standards Organization
IT	Information technology

The IT Infrastructure Library
Specification and Management of a Cable Infrastructure

LAN	Local Area Network
LED	Light emitting diode
LJU	Line Jack Unit
M & E	Mechanical and Electrical Engineering
MDF	Main distribution frame
MTBF	Mean time between or before failure(s)
MTBI	Mean time between incidents
MTTR	Mean time to repair
NLA	Net lettable area
OA	Office automation
OR	Operational Requirement
OTDR	Optical time domain reflectometer
PABX	Private automatic branch exchange
PRINCE	Projects IN Controlled Environments
PTO	Public Telecommunications Operator
RFI	Radio frequency interference
STP	Shielded twisted pair
TC	Telecommunications closet (see closet)
TJF	Test Jack Frame
UPS	Uninterruptible power supply
UTP	Unshielded twisted pair

Annex A
Glossary of terms

Definitions of terminology used in this module

10base2	ISO, LAN standard, 'thin Ethernet' or 'Cheapernet'
10base5	ISO, LAN standard, 'thick Ethernet'
10baseT	IEEE (1990) standard, 'Ethernet over UTP'
10baseF	Standard being developed by IEEE for Ethernet over fibre
ad-hoc cables	Cables installed for a particular purpose
availability	The proportion of time a service is available to users within agreed service times
bandwidth, cable	The range of signal frequencies that can be carried by a communications cable subject to specified conditions relating to signal loss and distortion
blown fibre	A method of installing fibre-optics into small tubes using compressed air
cable infrastructure	All building cables, including power for IT and building services, data, telephony, security and safety systems
cabling system	The cables supporting an application, such as voice or data
cellular space	Division of building floor space into self-contained office units; the direct alternative to open plan
circulation, primary	Areas of a building such as reception, lift, lobbies, main corridors
circulation, secondary	Passages between desks or work areas in an open plan or cellular office
closet (wiring, communication)	A room in which the primary, backbone telecommunications network is connected to the secondary horizontal distribution
coaxial cable	Cable consisting of two cylindrical conductors with a common axis, separated by dielectric material
connection	Interface between equipment and an infrastructure cable
contingency	planning to safeguard the IT infrastructure and to cope with, and recover from, an IT disaster.
cross connect	A frame holding termination blocks by which voice and data cables are interconnected, typically between backbone and local cabling

The IT Infrastructure Library
Specification and Management of a Cable Infrastructure

electromagnetic interference	Any electromagnetic disturbance or phenomenon that causes malfunctioning of electrical equipment or electronic equipment
ethernet	CSMA/CD local area network with a bus topology; commonly used as a generic name for ISO 8802/3 networks
fibre-optic cable	Communications cable incorporating fibre-optics as the carriers of the information, rather than copper conductors
fit-out	The process of installing services, floors, ceilings, wall coverings and furniture within an otherwise completed building shell.
frame room	Room in which connections are made between telecommunications cables, including cables connected to external services
gel filling	The use of gel, usually petroleum-based, to provide moisture protection of a cable by filling spaces in the construction
highly serviced zone	An area designed for use as, or for upgrade to, a closet or equipment room
horizontal cabling	See secondary cabling
hybrid cabling	Cable infrastructure using more than one type of medium
infrastructure project	The implementation of an IT infrastructure, partially or in its entirety
IT infrastructure	The hardware, software and computer-related communications that support the ongoing provision of IT services, including cabling for voice, power and data
local cabling	See secondary cabling
lux	Unit of intensity of illumination of a surface, equal to one lumen per square metre
media	Types of cable - for example, coaxial, twisted pair or fibre-optic
presentation	Group of connections; typically a floor box, where services can be accessed by a user
quantification	Calculation of number of connections and presentations for voice, data and power

Annex A
Glossary of terms

reliability	The capability of a functional unit to perform a required function under stated conditions for a stated period of time. This is usually measured in one of the following ways:
	* Mean time between incidents (MTBI).
	* The number of incidents over a given period.
resilience	Maintain or recover all or part of the IT infrastructure after a failure.
ribbon cable	Flat cable, consisting of individually insulated conductors lying parallel and bonded together
riser	Vertical shaft normally extending from the ground to the top floor and used to distribute services to all floors
RJ45	8-wire jack, used primarily for termination of UTP (Reference ISO 8877, BS 8877)
saturation cabling	Provision of access points to voice, data and power within convenient reach of all users, irrespective of the arrangement of the workplace
screed trunking	Cable trunking set into channels in a solid floor
secondary cabling	Cabling connecting equipment to a telecommunications closet
serviceability	The proportion of time that a system or unit is actually serviceable compared to the time that it is required to be serviceable
shield	A metallic layer wrapped around a cable to reduce interference from, and emission of, electromagnetic radiation
splitter	The means of connecting one cable to many cables (as in a tree topology)
stand-by generator	A diesel or gas turbine generator installed to provide electricity when the public supply fails
strategic cabling	Cabling that maximizes the benefits to be gained by investing in a flexible cable infrastructure that can meet the future demands of an organization's IT strategy
tactical cabling	Cabling to meet the demands of IT services as and when they arise

task lighting	Local lighting - for example, at a workplace - to assist with a specific task
terminal	The screen display and keyboard
Token Ring	Ring topology LAN, specified according to ISO 8802/5
uplighting	Indirect lighting where the light is reflected from the ceiling
user, end	The actual operator of IT equipment
user, senior	Manager representing a business area that uses IT systems for voice or data
work area	Individual work area, consisting of a screen display, keyboard, peripherals (for example, a printer), desk and chair.

Annex B - GOSIP Cabling Strategy

This annex reproduces Chapter 6 of the Supplement to GOSIP Version 3.1, first published in February 1990.

The GOSIP Supplement, issued with earlier versions of GOSIP, addressed those OSI and related issues which were not appropriate for inclusion in the GOSIP Specification as stable GOSIP subprofiles. It is not intended to issue a Supplement with future versions of the GOSIP Specification, for reasons outlined in 2.5.1. The guidance given in this annex remains valid for those organizations with a GOSIP-based network strategy and is included here for completeness and to obviate the need to refer to an outdated version of another publication.

The original work was produced by a Taskforce, under the auspices of the GOSIP project, comprising representatives from suppliers and UK government. The paper was strategic in nature and not intended to be a specification for procurement. It does, however, provide essential information on which to base a specification for a GOSIP-based strategic cabling infrastructure.

6. Cabling strategy

6.1 Introduction

This Chapter provides recommendations and guidance on strategic planning for a local cabling infrastructure to support LAN-based data communications.

It has become apparent that many user organisations urgently need guidance on how best to plan for a general-purpose cabling infrastructure to meet both data and voice communications requirements over a 10 to 15 year timeframe. Whereas such issues to some extent fall outside the primary role of GOSIP, it has been considered appropriate to provide some such guidance on an interim basis in the GOSIP Supplement as a necessary complement to the GOSIP LAN subprofile specifications, with particular reference to the interim GOSIP FDDI and CSMA/CD 10baseT LAN subprofile specifications in Chapter 5 of this GOSIP Supplement.

The description of cabling standards is not within the conventional scope of OSI, though the procurement of a cabling infrastructure may reference one or more of the existing GOSIP LAN subprofiles. Internationally agreed standards are not yet in place for the specification of structured cabling infrastructures. For these reasons, this guidance is placed in the GOSIP Supplement rather than in the main GOSIP Specification. Readers should note the general advice in Chapter 1 with respect to the contents of the GOSIP Supplement and the relationship of such contents to the primary GOSIP subprofiles.

LAN standards have not developed with a view to specifying a single communications medium over which all LANs can operate. It is considered unlikely that Departments and other users will install separate cable types to serve multiple LAN types. The choice of a general-purpose cabling infrastructure will therefore involve a compromise between practical implementation issues and standards-based procurement. At present, there is no strategic approach to LAN cabling which is based on approved international standards. The guidance in this Chapter indicates a preferred long-term strategic approach to cabling infrastructures, describes an architecture which has been agreed by a number of leading suppliers that is flexible enough to support a number of LAN types and minimizes migration problems. In addition, some interim approaches are also outlined.

Annex B
GOSIP cabling strategy

6.2 Status

The GOSIP V3.1 Cabling recommendations and guidance [GOSIP Cabling] contained in this Chapter reference Draft 10 of the proposed Commercial Building Wiring Standard from the Electronic Industries Association (EIA) [EIA/1907]. References to media and connector specifications are equivalent to those already included in relevant GOSIP LAN subprofiles and evolving international standards.

ISO JTC1/SC83/WG3 is conducting a study on Generic IT Cabling for Customer Premises. A 'top down' approach is being adopted to establish cabling needs based on current cabling practices and statistics, plus existing and emerging standards for local voice and data networks. The architectural model being considered is aligned with [EIA/1907]. Recommendations are currently being formulated with a view to proceeding to the development of an international standard for Generic IT Cabling which is expected to include topology, configuration options, media specifications and conformance test procedures.

It is intended that relevant guidance emerging from an appropriate international or European forum will be included in future versions of GOSIP.

Issues of future compatibility with respect to GOSIP Cabling are different from those which constrain GOSIP subprofiles such as MHS. Implementations of GOSIP subprofiles which are purchased at different times will be required to interwork and therefore to share a common set of features. A cabling infrastructure which is purchased should be sufficiently comprehensive to meet defined communications requirements over a specified timescale. These requirements will be localized to the buildings in which the infrastructure is in place. The fact that two buildings may have adopted different cabling architectures should not in itself constrain interworking provided the architectures can support the OSI services required by GOSIP subprofiles.

6.3 Scope

GOSIP Cabling addresses the generic cabling requirements for LAN-based communications services in a typical office environment as used in UK civil administration. These requirements are not unique and it is believed that GOSIP Cabling will have a wider applicability than in the UK Central Government environment alone. There are a number of issues, such as the physical layout of floor space within a particular building, provision of architectural drawings, etc, which are outside the scope of a generic document such as GOSIP. However, these issues require detailed and careful assessment and are discussed in section 6.8. GOSIP Cabling addresses a wide range of site configurations including multiple sites with a geographic extension up to 3,000m with 200 to 1,000,000 square metres of office space. The user population ranges from 50 to 50,000. Scenarios which fall below these minimum limits are not precluded from basing their requirements around GOSIP Cabling.

The cabling infrastructure which is installed should:

* Provide a level of protection of investment such that future networking requirements can be mapped onto the existing cable without the costly business of re-cabling;

* provide users with access to networked facilities irrespective of their geographical location;

* facilitate change control such that users can be relocated within a building and retain access to the facilities with which they are accustomed.

The cabling should be an enabling factor which allows organizations to meet existing and future business objectives rather than a constraining factor on future activity.

6.4 Architectural model

6.4.1 Topology

The building communication infrastructure must be capable of supporting long-term networking solutions which are expected to be highly distributed, and at the same time must be compatible with existing and intermediate requirements.

The adopted cabling architecture must therefore exhibit sufficient flexibility to support the graceful evolution of network solutions. It is also important to accommodate different rates of change within the same cabling infrastructure.

A conventional 'tree and branch' topography provides a powerful solution to the problem. The architecture shown in Fig F/CABLE/1 comprises a number of local cabling zones, each interconnected by a trunk. The points of interconnection may be referred to as nodes, where each

Annex B
GOSIP cabling strategy

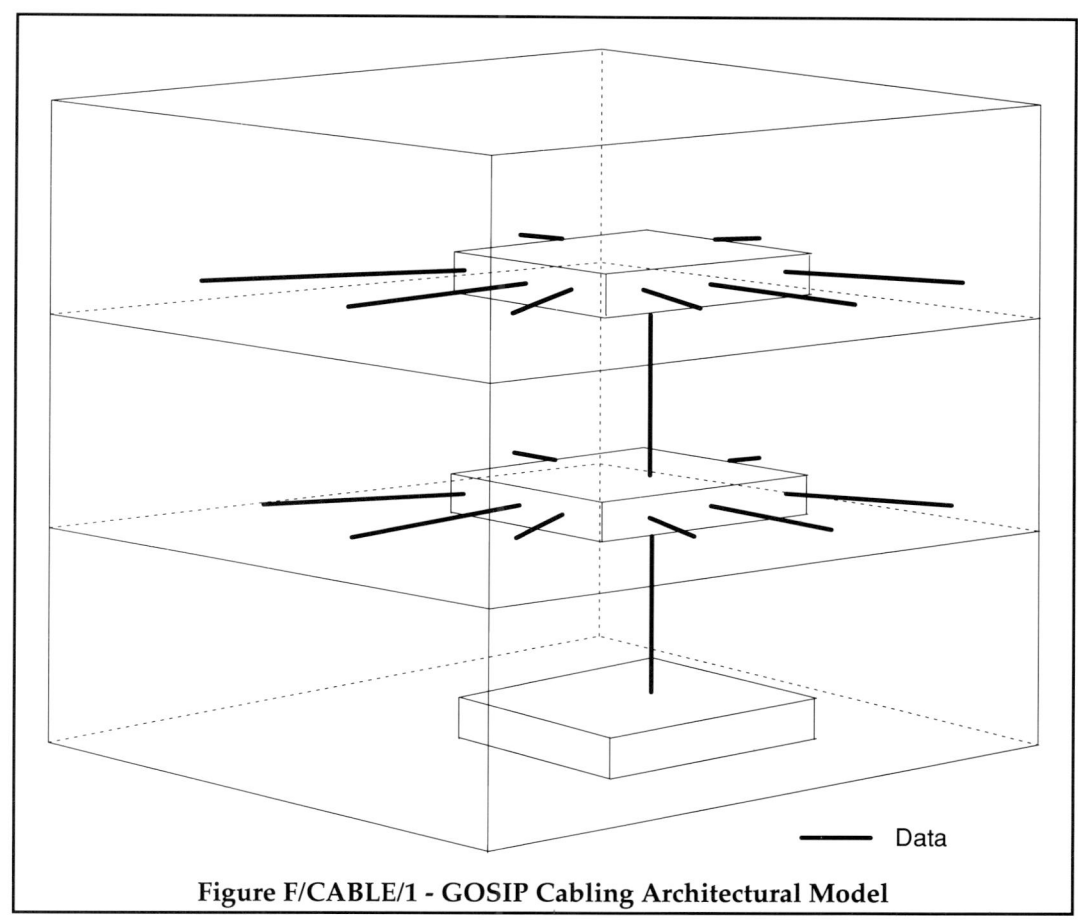

Figure F/CABLE/1 - GOSIP Cabling Architectural Model

node provides the key to network flexibility. Nodes can contain active functions (eg, repeaters, multiplexers) or, in their simplest form, be a point of passive interconnection between the two physical cabling domains. The approach shown in Fig F/CABLE/1 is essentially a 'ducting' architecture. Whilst this defines the geographical routing of each cable section, the overall logical configuration may be ring, bus, star, or point-to-point. The latter will be determined at a node, or a defined set of nodes.

6.4.2 The Local Cabling Zone

The Local Cabling Zone covers a convenient and manageable section of a building, which in practice may be an entire floor of a high-rise block. Taking the floorspace of a typical high-rise building to be 800 m² per floor (say 40m x 20m), then current UK Civil Service guidelines (as published in the Property Services Agency's Office Accommodation Statistics code) would allow for approximately 100 employees. Each of these 100 employees will have a telephone, and most are expected to own a data terminal in the foreseeable future.

The voice service requirements of the majority of users can be comfortably accommodated by relatively low bandwidth channels (approx. 64Kbit/s). In deciding how many cables will be required to connect each user to the information network, account must be taken of the fact that voice and data services will remain separate for many users for some time to come. A small proportion of users are expected to require sophisticated terminals/workstations on their desks in the foreseeable future, however this may increase dramatically in certain market sectors due to a demand for high definition image/graphics and even video services, plus an increase in disk-less workstations (greater than 10Mbit/s). The latter will have a significant effect on the choice of medium for local cabling.

It is essential that local cabling has a long installed life; that is, a minimum of 15 years, in order to provide a stable user environment. It is therefore vital to take full account of the growth in bandwidth over the installed lifetime of the local cable.

6.4.3 Saturation vs Dedicated Cabling

The traditional approach to communications cabling within a building has been based on the use of 'dedicated' connections. The cabling system has in this case been built around a 'snapshot' in time of the locations of each IT product. The number and routing of dedicated cable sections will change according to the population of resident users.

An approach based on dedicated cabling is understandably tempting due to its low entry cost. However the cost of installing and re-routing dedicated cables within the working environment is now recognized as a major consideration. The 'disturbance' factor must also be taken into account in the cost equation.

Based on the growth of IT in the office, and the need for users to be mobile, a more flexible approach to local cabling is emerging - saturation cabling. Saturation cabling simply

Annex B
GOSIP cabling strategy

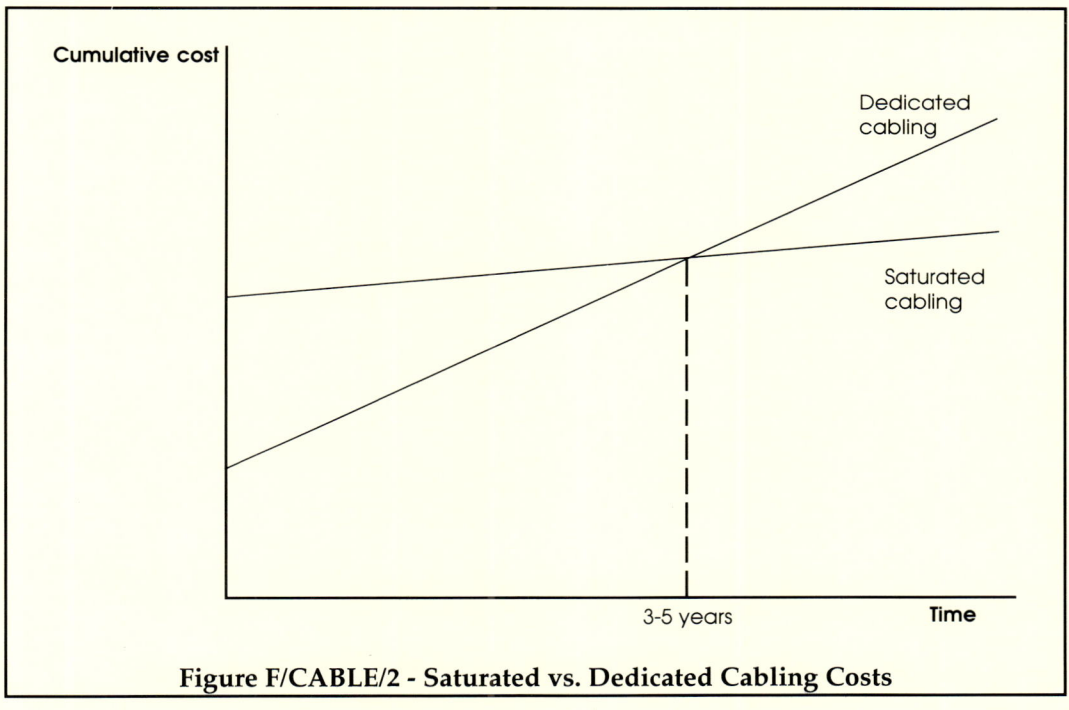

Figure F/CABLE/2 - Saturated vs. Dedicated Cabling Costs

provides network access points which are always within convenient reach of the user, irrespective of situation. The 'saturation' approach is somewhat akin to the local mains power distribution system, where sockets are provided at regular intervals throughout the workspace.

The initial cost of an IT network based on 'saturation' cabling will clearly be higher than that for 'dedicated' cabling, however studies indicate that cost of ownership is equivalent after a period of 3 - 5 years for many organisations. The saturation cabling approach then becomes more economical. The graph in Fig F/CABLE/2 indicates the typical results which have been obtained from studies of this issue.

A saturation density must be chosen which will represent the optimum balance of cost and convenience within the general office environment. A typical value would be 2m x 2m, though other constraints may result in a different value (eg, a 1.8m^2 grid maps neatly onto a 3 x 3 square of 600mm floor tiles).

6.4.4 Information Outlet

The information outlet is the network access point. It is some form of 'box' which contains such elements as power points and connections to voice and data communications services. The outlet will be positioned according to the degree of saturation which has been determined for the infrastructure. The outlets are a significant cost element of a cabling infrastructure and therefore must be designed to cope with future as well as existing requirements. It is recommended that sufficient physical space is left in such outlet 'boxes' to cope with optical fibre connectors. The outlet must be simple and clearly labelled. Separate connectors will be required for voice and data services in the shorter term, with the national standard telephone jack ([BS 6312] in the UK) providing the connection for voice. Ideally, a second co-located connector should provide a single outlet for the remaining communication services. In the longer term it is essential that this connector becomes a recognized industry standard to maximize the benefits of a universal cabling scheme. In the interim, it will be sufficient that all data services can be accessed in a building via a connector which is common throughout the building.

6.4.5 Nodes

Nodes provide the cabling infrastructure with the flexibility its users require. In its simplest form, a node will manage the cross-connection between local and trunk cabling. This represents a highly structured way of enabling dormant cable sections to be brought into service in the local zone, existing users to be re-located, or even disconnected.

Nodes also provide a convenient junction between the local working environment and the information trunk, or backbone. This 'junction' is important as it decouples the evolution of technologies applied in each of the cabling domains, thus allowing more frequent (and radical) changes in the trunk whilst maintaining stability in the local user environment. A node may also possess greater functionality. Signal amplifiers, repeaters and concentrators may be located at a network node - also bridges and gateways. The node will then become a logical 'junction' linking different protocols and transmission speeds.

Due to the strategic importance of the node, it is recommended that a small secure room (a telecommunications closet) be provided for cross-connect frames and equipment. The size of this room will be

Annex B
GOSIP cabling strategy

constrained by the number of users served by the room, the sophistication of the network technology in use and economic factors (floor rentals etc). Experience has shown that a room of say 2m x 3m should be sufficient to serve about 50-60 users. Restricting the size of this room is a false economy, especially as more communications services will be required by users, eg, at present most voice communications patching is performed at the PABX but in the future more patching functions will be required locally.

Returning to the previous example of the high-rise office block, a typical arrangement would require a node (and a telecommunications closet) somewhere on each floor. Resilience requirements may result in more than one node (and telecommunications closet) per floor.

6.4.6 Trunk Cabling

The information trunk must support the total communications requirement of a building. Fortunately, it will be easier in practice to evolve technology applied to the trunk system rather more rapidly than that used in the local zone. The life expectancy of trunk transmission systems can be 5 years or less, compared with 15 years or more for the local zone. It is therefore essential that ease of access to trunk cables be considered as part of the initial installation.

In the short-term, trunk systems will comprise separate cables for voice and data services. A traditional PBX trunk would be made up of individual circuits in multi-pair cables which would be cross-connected through to corresponding lines in the local zone. Today, the majority of data services would be provided by a LAN. Figure F/CABLE/3, overleaf, shows how these two cabling systems are overlaid, side-by-side, to form a trunk (it is recommended that voice and data services do not share the same cable sheath). In the longer-term, trunk systems must not only cater for greater bandwidths, but need also to accommodate the functional integration of communications services.

6.5 GOSIP LAN subprofiles

GOSIP Cabling references existing ISO and IEEE standards in order to specify certain properties of media and connectors. The references are consistent with those specified in the appropriate GOSIP LAN subprofiles.

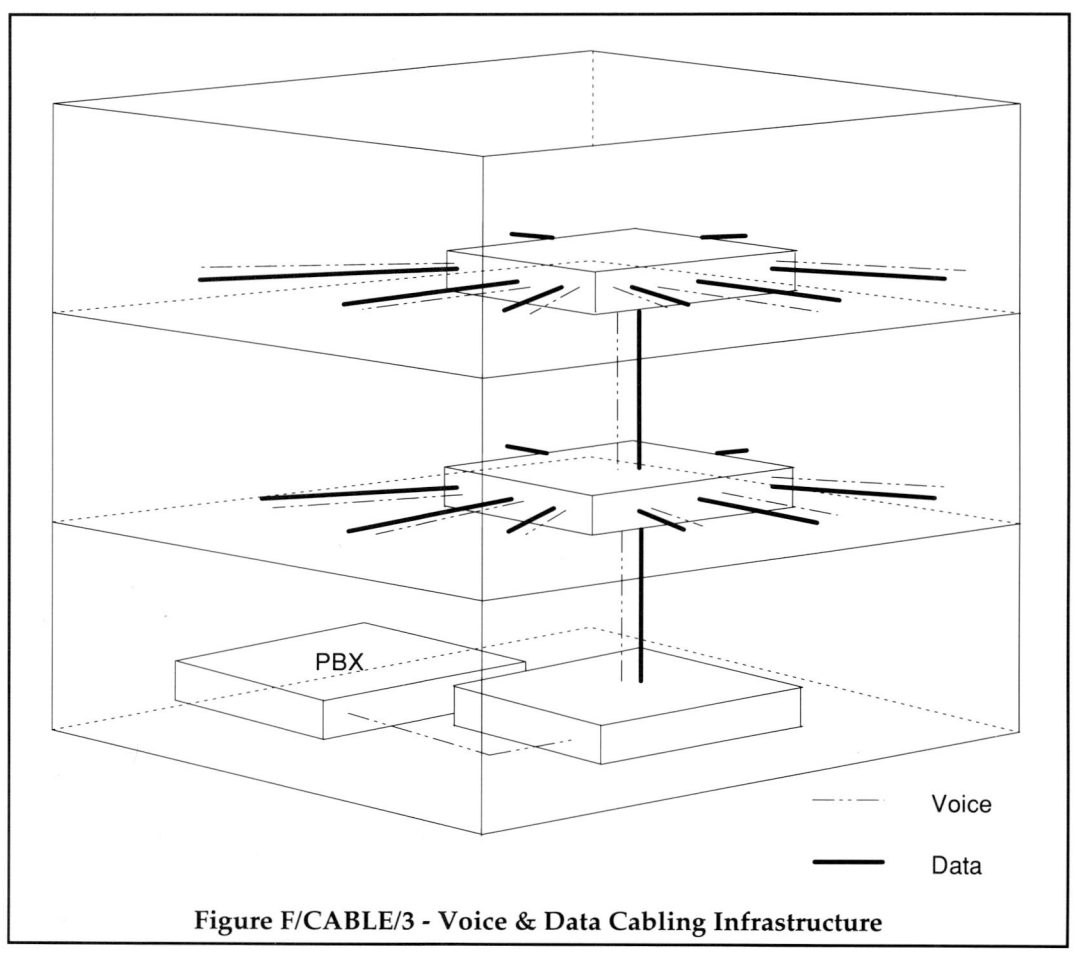

Figure F/CABLE/3 - Voice & Data Cabling Infrastructure

GOSIP V3.1 specifies five LAN options, each of which uses different media and connectors:

* CSMA/CD 10base5 - 'thick Ethernet';

* CSMA/CD 10base2 - 'thin Ethernet' or 'Cheapernet';

* CSMA/CD 10broad36 - 'Ethernet on broadband';

* CSMA/CD vendor-independent Fibre Optic Inter-Repeater Link (CSMA/CD FOIRL);

* Token Ring - 4 Mbits/sec on shielded twisted pair cabling.

Annex B
GOSIP cabling strategy

In addition, interim specifications are included in Chapter 5 of this GOSIP Supplement for those who wish to procure implementations of:

* CSMA/CD 10baseT - which uses unshielded twisted pair cabling (currently nearing approval within IEEE);

* FDDI - 100 Mbits/sec token passing ring based on fibre optic cabling (three of the four parts of this standard have reached IS or DIS status; the final part which deals with station management has yet to be finalized).

GOSIP Cabling defines an architecture which can support the following backbone implementations:

* CSMA/CD 10base5;

* CSMA/CD FOIRL;

* Token Ring;

* FDDI;

and the following local cabling implementations:

* CSMA/CD 10baseT;

* CSMA/CD 10base2;

* Token Ring;

* FDDI.

The specification of a cabling infrastructure to support other GOSIP LAN subprofiles is for further study.

GOSIP LAN subprofiles contain both a 'media' specification (the GOSIP LAN (MAC) subset) and the specification of the Network Service which should be achieved across the physical media up to and including the Transport Layer. A number of implementations can offer an appropriate Network Service over a media specification which is different from that included in the standards referenced by GOSIP. Examples of this are end systems directly attached to a fibre optic CSMA/CD LAN and Token Ring running over unshielded twisted pair cables.

Those purchasers who require their cabling infrastructure to support a number of different LAN types will therefore have to compromise either by:

* specifying a different media type than that defined within the GOSIP LAN subprofile, or

* supporting a number of different cable types within the infrastructure. This will lead to a large quantity of redundant cable installed and consequent cost penalties.

Purchasers who choose the less costly option of installing just one cable type should ensure that suppliers can provide the required support of the services and protocols to support the appropriate mode of OSI Network Service.

6.6 Functional description

6.6.1 Topology

The topology of the cabling infrastructure is described by the physical layout of the cables and other components. This topology must be flexible enough to meet a variety of application requirements and LAN types. GOSIP Cabling recommends that the backbone physical topology shall be a conventional hierarchical star as defined in [EIA/1907]. This topology is illustrated in Fig F/CABLE/4.

In this scenario, a main cross-connect (MCC) is at the top of the hierarchy and would typically be the point from which the backbone services for a number of buildings in a campus environment emanate. Each individual building is served by an intermediate cross-connect (ICC) from which the telecommunications closets (TCs) that serve each floor of the building emanate. Thus, the main cross connect can always be reached via a single cross connect which limits signal degradation for passive systems and simplifies administration. The backbone cable can therefore be considered to be the wiring which provides the physical and electrical interconnection between telecommunications closets, intermediate cross-connects and the main cross connect.

Annex B
GOSIP cabling strategy

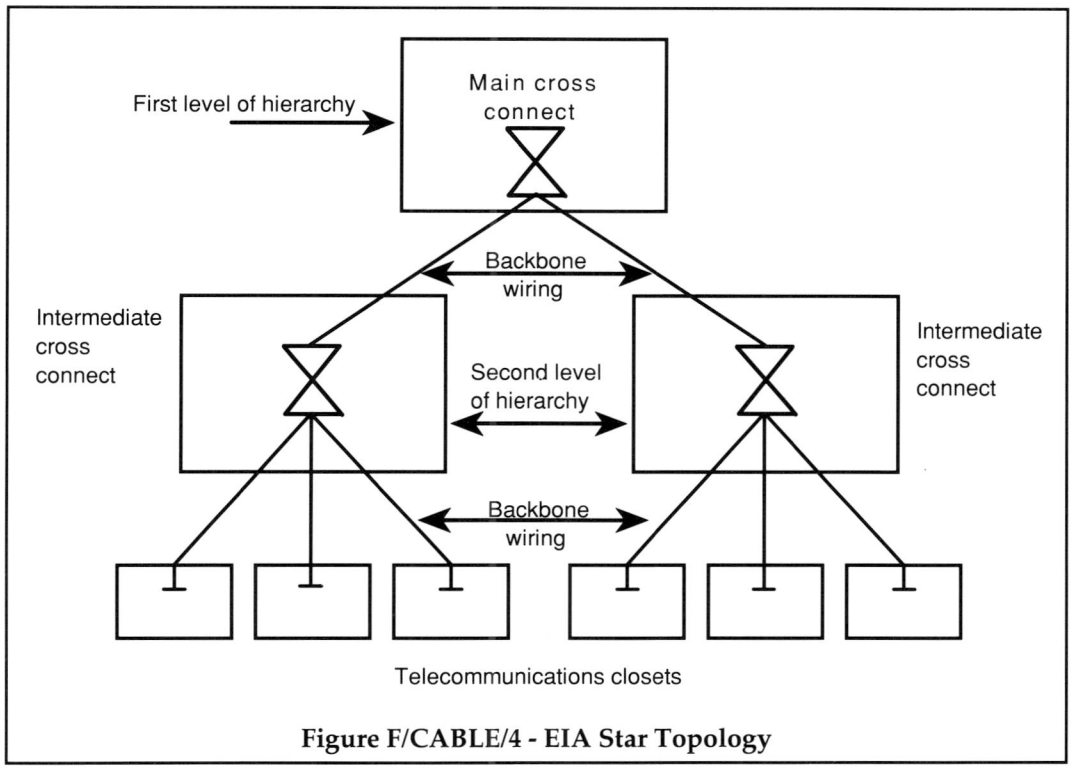

Figure F/CABLE/4 - EIA Star Topology

6.6.2 Configuration

The physical topology described above does not constrain the system to support only a logical star configuration, as the nature of interconnections and adapters in the cross connects and the telecommunications closets allow for bus, ring and tree configurations to be supported. These configurations are illustrated in Figures F/CABLE/5, F/CABLE/6 & F/CABLE/7. However, it is not recommended that implementations of CSMA/CD 10base5 in the backbone adopt this approach. In this case, a conventional bus approach is more cost-effective.

The IT Infrastructure Library
Specification and Management of a Cable Infrastructure

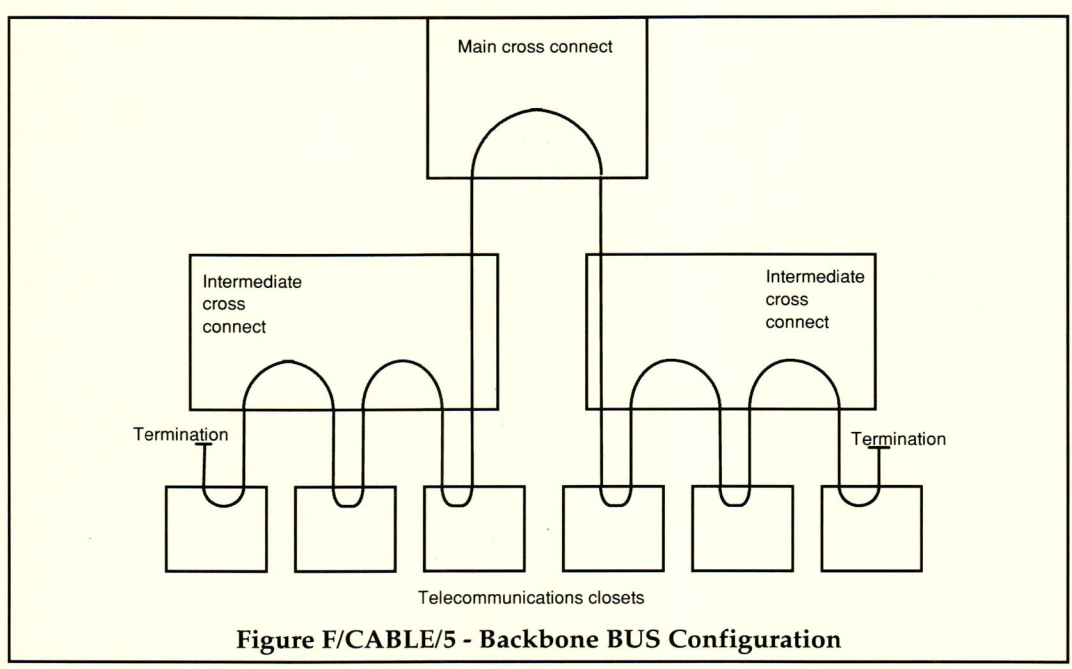

Figure F/CABLE/5 - Backbone BUS Configuration

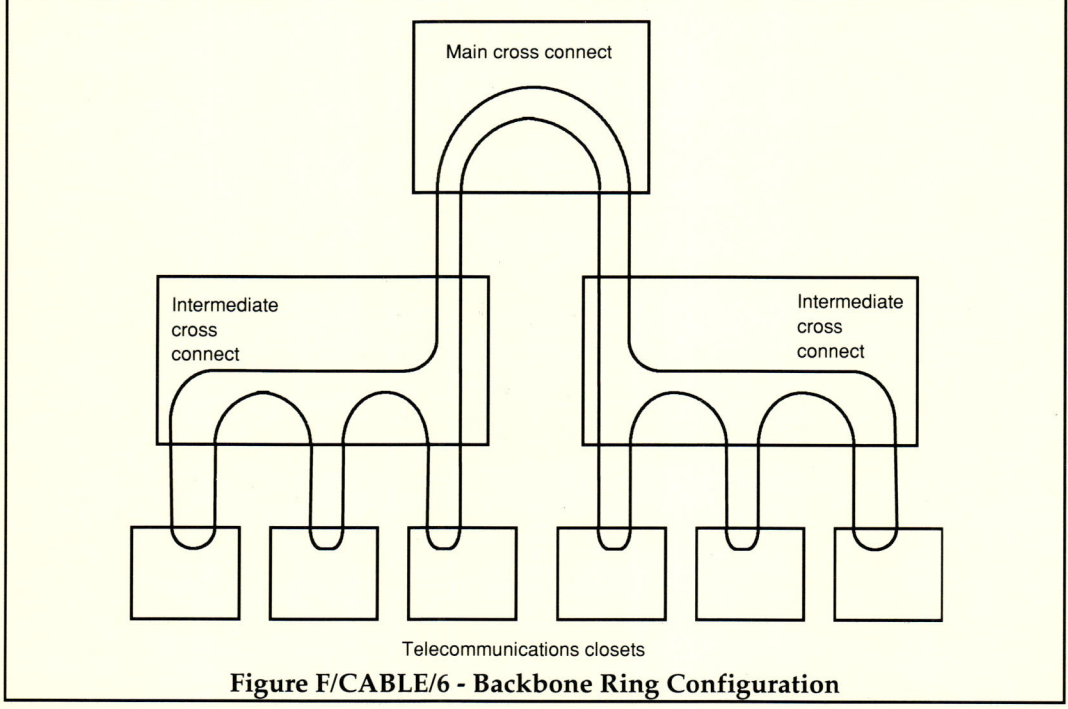

Figure F/CABLE/6 - Backbone Ring Configuration

Annex B
GOSIP cabling strategy

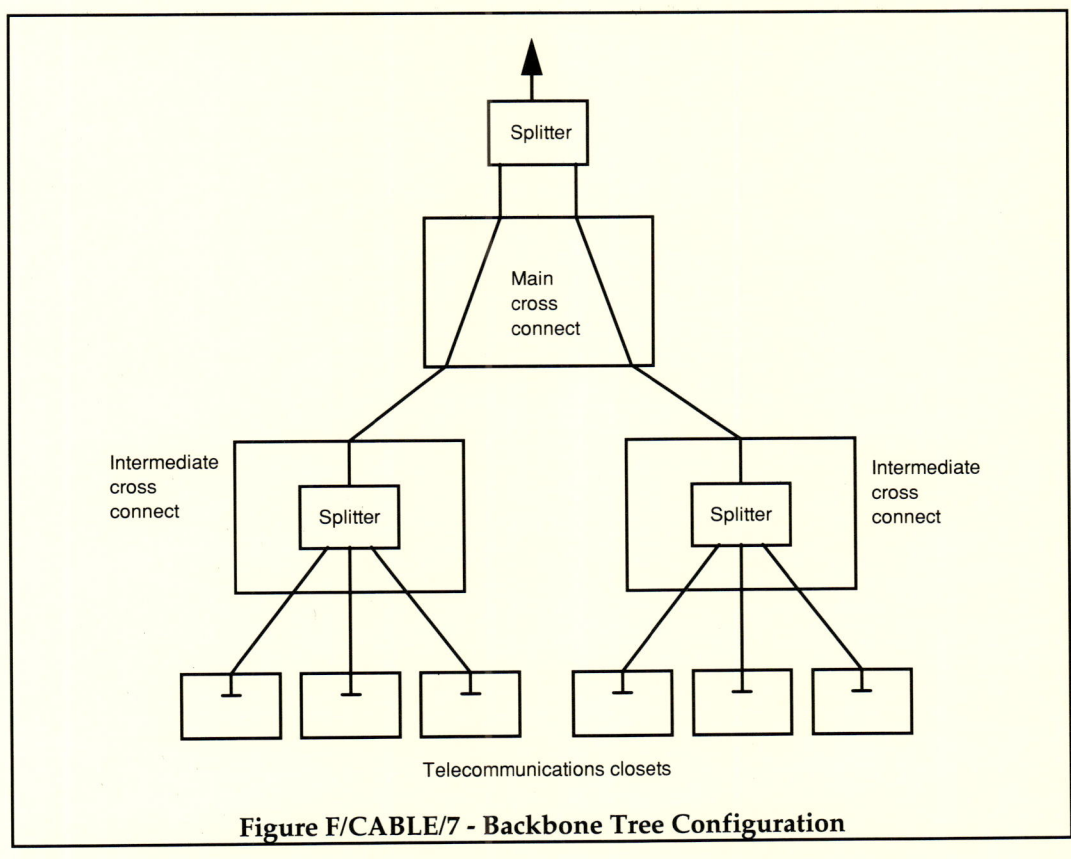

Figure F/CABLE/7 - Backbone Tree Configuration

6.6.3 Backbone Media Types

The recommended media types defined for the backbone in GOSIP Cabling are as follows:

* 100 ohm unshielded twisted pair (UTP) cable which shall meet all of the mandatory electrical and mechanical characteristics required by the GOSIP V3.1 CSMA/CD 10baseT LAN subprofile interim specification. This specification is adequate to meet the requirements for voice traffic. The use of UTP to carry LAN traffic in the backbone is not recommended. UTP is prone to electromagnetic interference in the backbone environment, which tends to be more pronounced than in the work area, and also suffers from more severe distance limitations than optical fibre, coaxial cabling and STP;

* 150 ohm shielded twisted pair (STP) cable which shall meet all of the mandatory electrical and mechanical characteristics required by the GOSIP V3.1 Token Ring LAN subprofile. The specification for STP in the base standards to which GOSIP refers is not as complete as desirable. Departments are advised to state their LAN requirements explicitly to suppliers (ie, Token Ring) and ensure that the cable is adequate for this purpose. Further work on an STP specification for Token Ring is underway in ISO/IEC JTC1/SC83/WG3;

* 50 ohm coaxial cable which shall meet all of the mandatory electrical and mechanical characteristics required by the GOSIP V3.1 CSMA/CD 10base5 LAN subprofile;

* 62.5µm/125µm multi-mode optical fibre which shall meet all of the mandatory optical and mechanical characteristics required by the GOSIP V3.1 FDDI LAN subprofile interim specification.

  [Note: The specification of other optical fibre types (eg 50/125 µm) is not included in GOSIP Cabling. While the current UK installed base of optical fibre is mostly 50/125 µm, the overall penetration of the medium remains small. It is therefore recommended that 62.5/125 µm cable be specified in new procurements as evolving fibre optic LAN standards are defined for the purposes of conformance tests, etc, to the 62.5/125 µm specification. Where a Department already has a large quantity of 50/125 µm installed, then GOSIP Cabling does not preclude a specification based on this cable type.]

The lengths of cable which are allowed for connection of the various elements of the cabling infrastructure (eg, main cross-connect to intermediate cross-connect) are listed in Table T/CABLE/1.

6.6.4 Local Cabling

Local cabling runs from the nodes located in the telecommunications closet to the information outlet described in section 6.4.4. The maximum cable length from the telecommunications closet to the outlet shall be 90m to ensure that the requirements of the LAN base standards can be accommodated whatever type of cable is employed. An additional 3m is allowed for the attachment of devices in the work area and 7m for patching in the telecommunications closet.

It is recommended that a star topology is adopted for local cabling. This does not limit the LAN types which can be supported to just CSMA/CD 10baseT as FDDI, Token Ring and CSMA/CD 10base2 can also be supported by this topology. It is the nature of the equipment which resides in the telecommunications closets which determines the LAN properties. This equipment could include CSMA/CD repeater sets, Token Ring Multistation-Access Units, distribution frames, patch panels, line-drivers and LAN bridges.

6.6.5 Local Cabling Media and Connector Types

The media types which are supported for local cabling are as follows:

* 4-pair 100 ohm UTP cable which shall meet all of the mandatory electrical and mechanical characteristics required by the GOSIP V3.1 CSMA/CD 10baseT LAN subprofile interim specification;

* 2-pair 150 ohm STP cable which shall meet all of the mandatory electrical and mechanical characteristics required by the GOSIP V3.1 Token Ring LAN subprofile;

* 50 ohm coaxial cable which shall meet all of the mandatory electrical and mechanical characteristics required by the GOSIP V3.1 CSMA/CD 10base2 LAN subprofile;

* 62.5/125 µm multi-mode optical fibre which shall meet all of the mandatory optical and mechanical characteristics required by the GOSIP V3.1 FDDI LAN subprofile interim specification. A minimum of 4 fibres is required to support FDDI. However, as the cable itself is one of the lower cost items in a cabling infrastructure, it is worth ensuring that sufficient fibres are installed both to meet future needs and to allow for a graceful migration to FDDI. For example, a fibre optic LAN installation may use FOIRL initially pending availability of final standard FDDI products. In such a case, it is likely that the transition phase will require both services to be operated in parallel.

The connector types used at the outlet will be different for each cable and are defined as follows:

* for 4-pair 100 ohm UTP: the data connector used shall be that specified in [BS8877] ('RJ45'), which shall meet all of the mandatory electrical and mechanical characteristics required by the GOSIP V3.1 CSMA/CD 10baseT LAN subprofile interim specification; the voice connector shall meet all of the mandatory electrical and mechanical characteristics of [BS6312];

* for 2-pair 150 ohm STP: the connector used shall be the media interface connector (MIC), which shall meet all of the mandatory electrical and mechanical characteristics required by the GOSIP V3.1 Token Ring LAN subprofile;

* for 50 ohm coaxial cable: the connector used shall be the BNC connector, which shall meet all of the mandatory electrical and mechanical characteristics required by the GOSIP V3.1 CSMA/CD 10base2 LAN subprofile;

* for 62.5/125 µm optical fibre: the connector used shall be the duplex connector, which shall meet all of the mandatory optical, electrical and mechanical characteristics required by the GOSIP V3.1 FDDI LAN subprofile interim specification.

> [Note: The interim specification for FDDI included in GOSIP V3.1 recommends that end systems are not directly attached to FDDI due to the high cost and low availability of FDDI concentrators at present (see Chapter 5). FDDI should instead be viewed as a high speed backbone which can interconnect a number of CSMA/CD and Token Ring LANs. GOSIP Cabling does not preclude proprietary 'fibre to the desk' solutions, although it is recommended that the cable and connector specified for such a solution shall also support FDDI station attachment requirements in the future. GOSIP Cabling does not preclude the use of another connector, but Departments should note that this may inhibit future migration by increasing re-termination costs]

The options outlined above are summarized in Table T/CABLE/1

Annex B
GOSIP cabling strategy

LOCAL CABLING	
Topology	Star
Configurations (as appropriate for requirements)	Star BUS Ring Tree
Cable types (as appropriate for requirements)	4-pair 100Ω UTP 2-pair 150Ω STP 50Ω coaxial 62.5µm/125µm multi-mode optical fibre
Maximum cable length	90m (see 6.6.4)
Connectors	**(8877)** (RJ45) for 4-pair 100Ω UTP **(8802/5)** MIC for 2-pair 150Ω STP **(8802/3)** BNC for 50Ω coaxial **(9314/3)** FDDI duplex for multi-mode optical fibre
BACKBONE CABLING	
Topology	Star BUS (for CSMA/CD 10base5 only)

Cable: Type	Maximum Allowable Length (m)		
	TC-MCC	**TC-ICC**	**ICC-MCC**
62.5/125µm multi-mode optical fibre	2000	500	1500[1]
150Ω STP	1200	500	700
50Ω coaxial	1000	500	500

1. When the TC-ICC distance is less than the maximum, the ICC-MCC distance can be increased accordingly to a maximum of 2000m.

Table T/CABLE/1 - Summary of Recommendations

6.6.6 Management

In order to ensure the efficient administration of the infrastructure, adequate management procedures should be established by the supplier which include, for example, the labelling and colour coding of the components of the infrastructure. The format and content of the cabling documentation should be specified by the Department. This may be a paper-based solution or reference may be made to one of a number of IT support packages which can be used to manage a cabling infrastructure.

This documentation should comprise:

* detailed floor plans showing the layout of telecommunications closets, intermediate and main cross-connects and the equipment therein (ie, patch panels, repeaters, etc);

* a labelling scheme to ensure that each element of the infrastructure can be uniquely identified. This should be sufficiently comprehensive that the identifier of the information outlet should identify the telecommunications closet which serves the outlet and locate the appropriate patch panel and patch panel port which serves that outlet. If Departments already have an established scheme in place, then this should be stated to suppliers as a requirement for the new infrastructure. Alternatively, Departments should ask that suppliers explain the detail of their own labelling systems;

* a colour coding system which uniquely identifies cables from the TC to the information outlet, from the ICC to the TC, and from the MCC to the ICC. Records of cable types, lengths and gauge should also be maintained.

Procedures should be established to ensure that the records are maintained so as to provide an up to date representation of the infrastructure.

6.7 Implementation issues

A number of different configurations can be achieved using the GOSIP Cabling recommendations based on a combination of the different backbone and local cabling specifications detailed in section 6.6. These configurations are summarized in Table T/CABLE/2. The configurations are defined as:

* Strategic (S), where the infrastructure should be regarded as a major investment which will meet long-term data and voice communication requirements over a 15 year timescale;

* Interim (I), where there are certain immediate tactical benefits because proven and well established products are readily available, but long term migration problems may be encountered;

Annex B
GOSIP cabling strategy

* Future (F), where the options may be applicable for future strategy, but stable base standards do not yet exist and no GOSIP specifications have yet been developed;

* Undefined (-), where the options are considered inadequate for a major long-term investment.

Medium	Services Supported	Backbone	Local
UTP	CSMA/CD 10baseT Token Ring Voice	- - S	S F S
STP	Token Ring	I	I
Coaxial	CSMA/CD 10base5 CSMA/CD 10base2	I -	- I
Optical Fibre	CSMA/CD FOIRL FDDI CSMA/CD 10baseF Token Ring	I S - F	- F F F

Table T/CABLE/2 - Implementation Configurations

6.7.1 Backbone Cabling

6.7.1.1 Strategic

The strategic direction for backbone cabling should reflect the increasing data traffic which such media will have to carry as user requirements demand higher bandwidths to meet a larger number of increasingly sophisticated applications. The recommended medium to meet this requirement is the fibre optic cable defined in 6.6.3. The FDDI standard is the most complete of any of the fibre optic LAN standards and an interim specification is included in this version of GOSIP. The mapping of the ring configuration required by FDDI onto the physical star topology is described in 6.6.2.

6.7.1.2 Interim

Users may wish to adopt fibre optic cable as the strategic medium but prefer to use a more mature standard without incurring migration problems in the future. The CSMA/CD Inter-Repeater Link could be specified in the backbone to run over the same medium and same physical topology as would later be required by FDDI. In this case the mapping outlined in Fig F/CABLE/5 in 6.6 would be required.

Departments are advised to ensure that suppliers state how a possible future migration to FDDI could be achieved in practice to ensure that new cable runs are not required. This is an example of where not all of the fibres installed in a building would necessarily be used in the first instance.

Where a Department requires a cost-effective cabling infrastructure in the short term only (eg, if there are plans to relocate to a different building) conventional coaxial cable (for CSMA/CD 10base5) or shielded twisted pair (for Token Ring) would be an adequate solution.

6.7.1.3 Future

No standards have yet emerged for the use of Token Ring over fibre optic media, although there are proprietary products available which will provide this facility. It is questionable whether Departments would base a future backbone strategy over a 4 (or even 16) Mbit/sec LAN when FDDI will offer 100 Mbit/sec.

6.7.1.4 Undefined

The use of CSMA/CD 10base2 in the backbone would fail to meet the distance requirements detailed in Table T/CABLE/1.

Users who may wish to use CSMA/CD over fibre optic media in the backbone should reference the GOSIP V3.1 CSMA/CD Fibre Optic Inter-Repeater Link specification.

The use of UTP in the backbone is discussed in section 6.6.3.

6.7.2 Local Cabling

6.7.2.1 Strategic

Local cabling should be unobtrusive, easily managed and flexible in terms of the LAN types which can be supported. the cable which best meets these requirements is the unshielded twisted pair cable referenced in 6.6.5. This cable can support both CSMA/CD and Token Ring LANs, although complete conformance to the GOSIP V3.1 Token Ring subprofile strictly requires the use of shielded twisted pair cabling. Section 6.10 discusses the procurement specification of a Token Ring LAN running on UTP. The specification of a 4Mbit/sec Token Ring over UTP is now underway in IEEE 802.5. UTP will meet the requirements of those Departments who choose CSMA/CD as a strategic direction or who wish to maintain a flexible approach.

6.7.2.2 Interim

Departments who choose Token Ring as the strategic direction for their LAN requirements may wish to use STP and maintain full conformance with the GOSIP Token Ring LAN subprofile.

Short term benefits may accrue from the use of coaxial media to provide CSMA/CD 10base2. Products to meet this specification are readily available from a large number of suppliers. However the medium offers no technical benefits over twisted pair.

6.7.2.3 Future

Some suppliers now offer 'fibre to the desk' solutions using non-standard mappings of CSMA/CD and Token Ring over fibre optic cable. Standards are under development in this area but such solutions will give identical bit rates to those using conventional twisted pair media. They may however provide some benefits in electrically 'noisy' environments. Procurement of such solutions is discussed in section 6.9.

As noted earlier, the GOSIP V3.1 FDDI LAN subprofile interim specification does not recommend direct workstation attachment to FDDI. However, in the longer term many high bit rate requirements (eg, document image processing) will benefit from the higher throughput of FDDI and this approach may be the basis for such a long term strategy.

6.7.2.4 Undefined

The CSMA/CD Fibre Optic Inter-Repeater Link is not appropriate in the local zone. The CSMA/CD 10base5 standard cannot meet the local cable length requirements of GOSIP Cabling for station attachment.

6.7.3 Sizing of Local Populations

The ideal scenario on which the GOSIP Cabling model would be overlaid envisages a single telecommunications closet with sufficient capacity to serve all the users on a single floor. Only backbone cable would run between floors from the telecommunications closet to the intermediate cross connect. This scenario is illustrated in Figure F/CABLE/8. An ideal figure for the number of attached data communications devices which a typical TC would support would be 50. This is not a technical constraint but represents a 'manageable' figure.

The IT Infrastructure Library
Specification and Management of a Cable Infrastructure

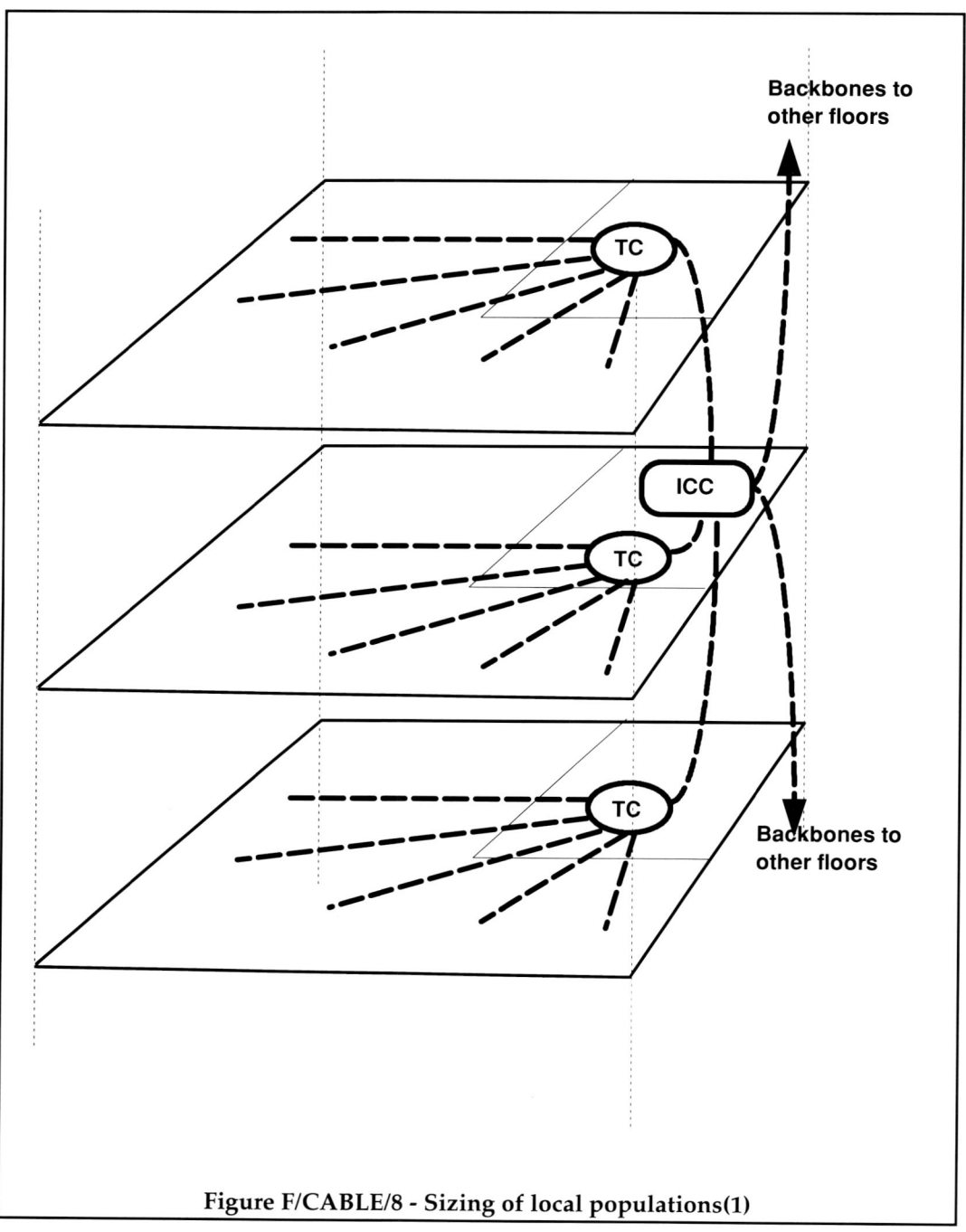

Figure F/CABLE/8 - Sizing of local populations(1)

Annex B
GOSIP cabling strategy

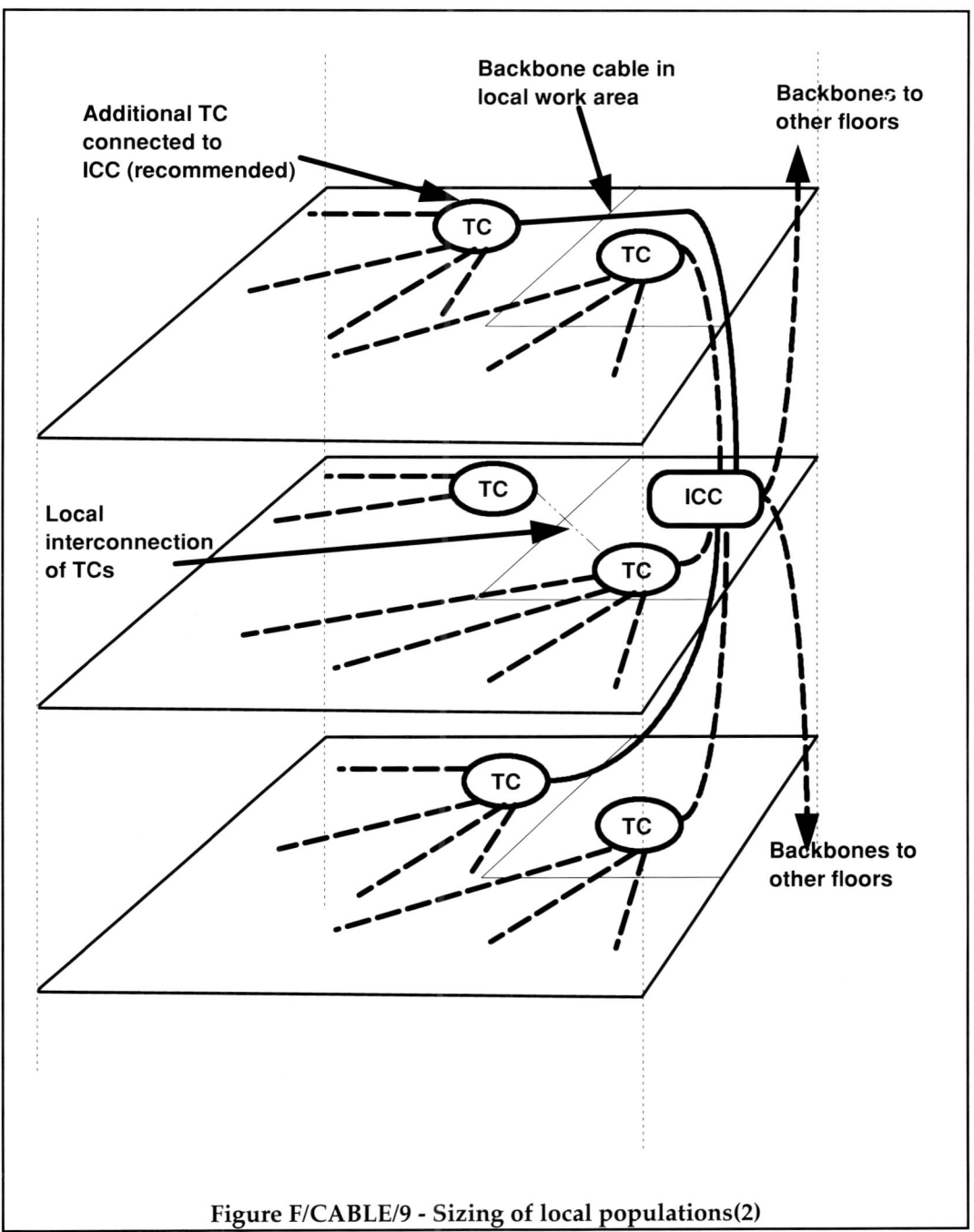

Figure F/CABLE/9 - Sizing of local populations(2)

There may be circumstances where the floor area is so large that supporting all devices from a single TC is not a feasible solution or becomes a management headache. In this situation more than one TC may be sited on an individual floor. This has the undesirable consequence of backbone cabling intruding in the local domain. It is therefore imperative that the cable connecting the TCs is as accessible as possible. The additional TC should ideally be connected to the ICC though the local interconnection of TCs is not ruled out. This scenario is illustrated in Figure F/CABLE/9.

Where the floor area is small, the use of one TC per floor may not be cost-effective. In this case it is possible that a number of floors are served by one TC or, in the case of very small buildings, the whole building. This scenario is illustrated in Figure F/CABLE/10.

Whatever the size of the telecommunications closet, sufficient space should be made available in the immediate vicinity of the closet to house the large amount of local cabling which will emanate from this point. The closets should be located near the risers which house the backbone cable but should be separate from them.

6.8 Procurement

The scope of GOSIP Cabling precludes a simple reference in a requirements specification to 'conformance to GOSIP Cabling'. GOSIP Cabling offers generic advice on cabling and highlights issues which should be addressed in all procurements. However, the issues covered in this Chapter are not exhaustive and situation-specific requirements will always remain.

It is recommended that Departments who wish to procure a cabling infrastructure should consult this Chapter for initial guidance and make references to relevant subsections as considered appropriate. Particular consideration should be given to the issues discussed in 6.6 and 6.7.

Some of the more important non-generic issues are outlined below.

Annex B
GOSIP cabling strategy

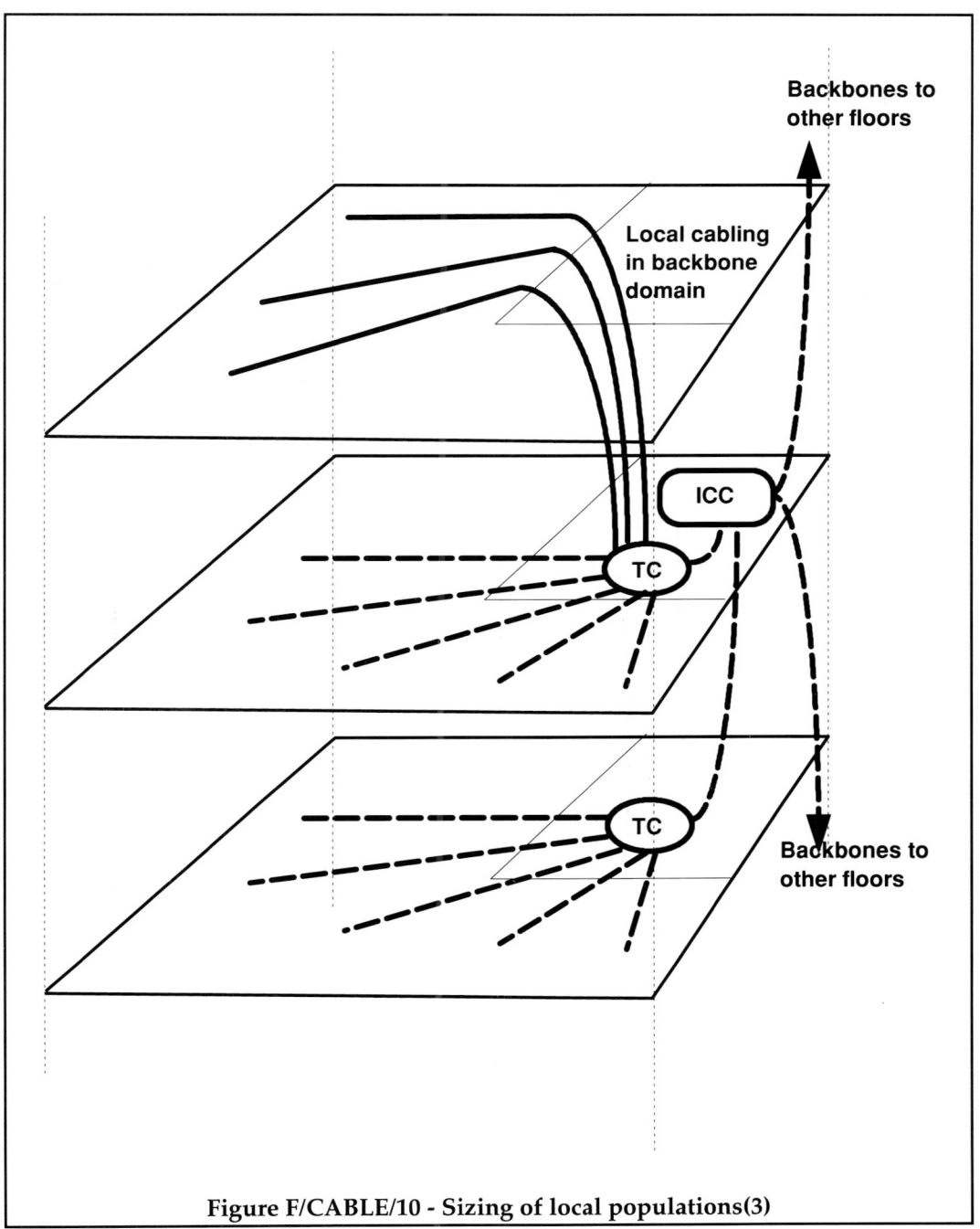

Figure F/CABLE/10 - Sizing of local populations(3)

The IT Infrastructure Library
Specification and Management of a Cable Infrastructure

6.8.1 Extent of Proposed Work

It must be stated clearly to the supplier how much of the proposed infrastructure must be supplied. This may include:

* cables;
* connectors;
* termination of cables;
* labelling of cables & components;
* cable trays, conduits and trunking;
* distribution frames and patch panels;
* testing and certification of the infrastructure.

6.8.2 Building-specific Requirements

The constraints imposed by the physical dimensions and layout of the building will be a critical factor in determining the success of the implementation.

The key issues to address in this area include:

* the provision of architectural plans including floor layouts;
* co-ordination with other building services eg power distribution, air conditioning;
* location and size of risers;
* location and size of rooms to house the TCs, ICCs and MCC;
* description of any false floors or ceilings which may be employed;
* the required saturation density of data and voice outlets.

6.8.3 Existing & Proposed IT & Voice Systems

These will be a major constraint in determining the cable types which are selected for the cabling infrastructure.

6.8.4 Installation & Test Procedures

It is important that the supplier either abides by existing requirements which have been adopted by the Department or that the supplier describes fully the procedures he proposes to employ.

6.8.5 Earthing

The supplier should ensure that all necessary components of the infrastructure are earthed and should state what these components are in any response to a requirements specification.

6.8.6 Maintenance/Serviceability

Serviceability criteria and maintenance requirements should be specified.

6.9 Non-standard media

An important consideration when specifying a cabling infrastructure is the LAN types which must be supported. If a Department has decided which GOSIP LAN subprofiles it should adopt strategically, then it should be a requirement that the proposed cabling infrastructure should support those LAN subprofiles. Alternatively, if a Department has no clear position on the preferred LAN types, the infrastructure should be sufficiently flexible to support a range of LAN implementations.

The GOSIP LAN subprofiles contain a medium-dependent specification at the Physical Layer, a medium access control (MAC) sublayer specification and a medium-independent specification. There are two medium-independent specifications, depending on whether the LAN provides the Connection-mode Network Service (CONS) or the Connectionless-mode Network Service (CLNS). For a discussion of these issues, refer to Chapters 4 and 5 of the GOSIP Procurement Handbook Chapters on LANs and Internetworking.

Certain LAN configurations are allowed in GOSIP Cabling which are not defined in the GOSIP V3.1 LAN subprofiles, viz.:

* the use of UTP for Token Ring in the local cabling zone;

* the use of optical fibre for Token Ring in the backbone and local cabling zone;

* the use of optical fibre for CSMA/CD in the local cabling zone.

Departments which wish to procure such solutions are advised to seek guidance on how to specify correctly the OSI Network and Transport Service across such LANs.

IT Infrastructure Library
Specification and Maintenance of a Cable Infrastructure

Comments sheet

CCTA hopes that you find this book both useful and interesting. We will welcome your comments and suggestions for improving it.
Please use this form or a photocopy, and continue on a further sheet if needed.

From:

                Name

        Organization

             Address

           Telephone

COVERAGE
Does the material cover your needs?
If not, then what additional material would you like included.

CLARITY
Are there any points which are unclear?
If yes, please detail where and why.

ACCURACY
Please give details of any inaccuracies found.

If more space is required for these or other comments, please continue overleaf.

IT Infrastructure Library
Specification and Maintenance of a Cable Infrastructure

OTHER COMMENTS

Return to: Environmental Infrastructure Services
CCTA
Riverwalk House
157 - 161 Millbank
LONDON SW1P 4RT

Further information

Further information on the contents of this module can be obtained from:

Environmental Infrastructure Services
CCTA
Riverwalk House
157-161 Millbank
London SW1P 4RT

Tel.   071-217 3068   (GTN 217 3068)

Further information on the contents of the IT services management modules can be obtained from:

IT Infrastructure Management Services
CCTA
Gildengate House
Upper Green Lane
Norwich NR3 1DW

Tel.   0603-694854   (GTN 3014 4854)

The price of this publication has been set to make a contribution to the costs incurred by CCTA in preparing the copy.

Printed in the United Kingdom for HMSO.
Dd. 0292688, 7/91, C7, 3390/3, 5673, 155910.